The Optimum State Guide to Tax Deed and Lien Investing

BE FREE UNIVERSITY

Web Site: https://befreeuniversity.com **Phone:** 855.5BE.FREE

Be Free University, LLC

Privacy Policy and Earnings Disclaimer

The information ideas and suggestions contained herein have been developed from sources including publications and research that are considered and believed to be reliable but cannot be guaranteed insofar as they apply to any particular investor moreover because the laws and procedures pertaining to property tax law are never static but ever changing and vary dramatically from state to state.

You should always familiarize yourself with the specific laws and procedures pertaining to property tax law. This book is sold with the understanding that neither the publisher nor the Authors are engaged in rendering legal investment or accounting information, nor are they offering professional services. If legal advice or expert assistance is required the services of a competent professional should be sought out when necessary.

The author specifically disclaims any liability or risk personal or otherwise incurred as consequence directly or indirectly of the use and application of any of the techniques or contents of this book.

Individual results will vary greatly and in accordance to your input, determination, access to financing, hard work, and ability to follow directions.

Your level of success in attaining the results claimed in our materials depends on the time you devote to the program, the amount of finances you have access to, the ability to obtain financing including but not limited to access to credit, the knowledge and various skills in real estate. Because each of these

 **BE FREE** UNIVERSITY

Web Site: https://befreeuniversity.com **Phone:** 855.5BE.FREE

factors differ, we simply cannot and refuse to offer any kind of guarantee to your success or the amount of income you may be able to earn. In addition, we are not responsible for any legal claims, suites, or consequences of taking any legal action, purchases, acquisitions or the like resulting from any methods learn in this publication.

Be Free University has taken every effort to ensure this information is accurate and the best training possible. Therefore, we make no claims you will earn any money using the techniques and ideas in these materials. Examples in these materials are not to be interpreted as a promise or guarantee of earnings.

How To Contact Us

Should you have other questions or concerns about these privacy policies, please call us at 855-5BE-FREE or send us an email at: support@befree.university

Contents

Introduction 6

The Best Investment In The World 7

Tax Deed State List 15

Alaska 15

Arkansas 17

California 19

Idaho 20

Kansas 22

Maine 23

Massachusetts 26

Michigan 27

Minnesota 28

Nevada 29

New Mexico 30

New York 31

North Carolina 33

North Dakota 34

Ohio 36

Oklahoma 38

Oregon 42

Utah 43

Virginia 44

Washington 45

Wisconsin 46

Tax Lien States 49

Alabama 49

Arizona 52

Colorado 54

Web Site: https://befreeuniversity.com **Phone:** 855.5BE.FREE

Illinois 57

Iowa 61

Kentucky 63

Louisiana 65

Maryland 67

Mississippi 69

Missouri 71

Montana 75

Nebraska 76

New Jersey 78

Rhode Island 82

South Dakota 84

Vermont 88

West Virginia 89

Wyoming 91

Hybrid States 93

Hybrid State List 93

Connecticut 94

Delaware 98

Florida 100

Georgia 104

Hawaii 106

Indiana 107

Pennsylvania 110

South Carolina 111

Tennessee 115

Texas 117

Who Is Financial Moses? 121

Web Site: https://befreeuniversity.com **Phone:** 855.5BE.FREE

Introduction

Learning Tax Liens and Deeds has allowed me to change my life where me or my children will never have to work again. I believe tax liens and deeds are the best investment on the face of the earth. So, congratulations on taking your first step to learning more about this investment and how you too can change your life if you work hard and apply the principles with diligence and consistency.

Today almost everyone is a guru of some sort. Well, I'm not a guru. I'm an investor who has been successful with obtaining over 130 properties. My students have purchased over 3000 properties across America. No other educator or course creator can make these claims no matter how long they have been in business. I have also had the opportunity to train some of the most prolific educators who also have chosen to teach Tax Liens and Deeds.

I know without a shadow of doubt that Tax Liens and Deeds are the best investment in America. Today there are so many ways to get started in real estate but Tax Liens and Deeds allow you to invest with no credit and very little capital. The only thing you need to be successful is knowledge.

This program is designed to give you the same opportunity for success my students and I have had. I understand everyone will not have the same results as individuals have different drive, work ethic, access to capital, and just plain determination to be successful.

I can make you this guarantee: there is nothing stopping you from being successful with Tax Liens and Deeds other than you. I challenge you today to not accept anything other than success.

Tax Liens and Deeds will allow you to purchase properties for as little as $500. I know because I have purchased several properties for $500 and so have my students. Today, many of these same properties are worth more than $100,000.

I know you may be asking yourself what kind of house you can buy for $500. What if I told you I have purchased over 20 properties with tenants in them for $500 or less. These properties were livable and not raggedy shacks. On the other hand, I have purchased some shacks as well that I knew had potential to cash

 **BE FREE** UNIVERSITY   **Web Site:** https://befreeuniversity.com **Phone:** 855.5BE.FREE

flow and have a good after repair value. (ARV)

What I'm telling you is that there is another way to get into real estate without having to use your credit, tens of thousands of dollars or having years of knowledge to be successful. Don't get me wrong it is so much easier when you do have these things but not having them does not prevent success with Tax Liens and Deeds.

There are several reasons to invest in Tax Liens and Deeds.
Many people invest for the double digit guaranteed returns that is managed by the local government; however, I invest for the properties. No matter what your reason for investing is there is no other opportunity like Tax Deeds and Liens.

The Best Investment In The World

I personally believe there are 5 reasons why Tax Liens and Deeds are the best investment in the world.

1. **It is the oldest investment in America**
   Tax lien and deed sales are the oldest investment in America. Tax Liens and Deeds were founded in the late 1700's which predates some of the most trusted investments we all know today. Tax Liens and Deeds predate the Federal Reserve System founded in 1913 and the Stock Exchange founded in 1817. Any investment that has been around this long I think is pretty secure as an investment.

2. **Double digit returns**
   Forbes magazine says that a 6% return is a good return. Well, Tax Liens and Deeds surpass this in many cases by at least 300%. Tax Liens and Deeds are typically at least 10% but can range up to 36% depending on the state the investor invest in. In addition, an investor can get up to 50% in the state of Texas by getting 25% returns every 6 months by investing in non-homestead properties.

3. **Your returns are fixed**
   In a up market the investor is happy however in a down market the investor

 **BE FREE** UNIVERSITY

Web Site: https://befreeuniversity.com **Phone:** 855.5BE.FREE

is worried and ready to pull his hair out. Unlike the stock market that has so many ups and downs it leaves the investor always wondering how their investment is performing, with Tax Liens and Deeds the investor has a fixed rate of return. No matter what happens in the market or the economy the investor will always know what their return is and when it will mature. In most cases an investor's return will be at least double digits.

4. **My investment is secured by real estate**

   There is no other investment in the world that is secured other than Tax Liens, therefore Tax Liens almost gives guaranteed investment (only in some cases is the investment not guaranteed). Most of the time a tax lien investment is secured by the property that is secured by a lien. This means that no matter what the investor wins. If the investor does not get their double-digit return (most states) then the investor gets the house. We have mastered how to get the house about 80% of the time and I have taught this strategy to my students.

5. **Managed by the government**

   This investment is not managed by some flyby night investor who may take off with your money or lead you into a Ponzi scheme. No, Tax Liens and Deeds are managed by the government of each state. There is actual state law that has passed the house and senate and signed by the governor. This gives me security in knowing that my investment is safe.

As I examine the above reason, I can't help but to get excited. In addition, when I compare Tax Liens and Deeds to other investments, I get even more excited. Look how they perform compared to some of the most known investments in the country.

BE FREE UNIVERSITY   **Web Site:** https://befreeuniversity.com   **Phone:** 855.5BE.FREE

	Avg Return 10 Years	High Risk	Guaranteed Collateral	Broker Cost
Tax liens	10% - 50%	No	Yes	No
Stocks	7.8%	Yes	No	Yes
Mutual Funds	8.0%	No	No	Yes
Bonds	6.6%	No	No	No
Annuities	5.5%	Yes	No	Yes
Gold	7.7%	Yes	No	Yes
401 K	4%	Yes	No	No
Real Estate	10.6%	Yes	No	Yes

Hands down Tax Liens and Deeds win when compared to other investments. There have a better 10-year average, less risk, guaranteed collateral and no broker cost. Tax Liens and Deeds are by far superior to any other investment I have ever seen. Not to mention Tax Liens and Deeds took me from homeless to owning over 100 properties (at one time) and a net worth of over 10 million dollars in as little as 9 years.

Let's Explain What a Tax Lien Is

A tax lien is a legal claim against a property that occurs when the property's owner fails to pay government taxes. Tax liens are placed by the city or county in which the property is located, and act as a legal claim to the property for the unpaid amount. Properties with a tax lien on them can't be sold or refinanced until the taxes are paid and the lien is removed.

After a tax lien is placed on a property, the local government issues a tax lien certificate that details the amount owed. These certificates are then auctioned off to investors. The amount that a tax lien might sell for depends on the specifics of the property.

Web Site: https://befreeuniversity.com **Phone:** 855.5BE.FREE

Tax lies are different than a mortgage lien as a mortgage lien give a lender claim to your property until you pay the mortgage in full. However, a tax lien, gives the government or to tax lien investor claim to the property.

Tax lien investing is necessary since approximately $21 billion in delinquent property taxes are unpaid each year. This means there is plenty of inventory for everyone as Tax Liens are a booming business.

There is a difference in purchasing Tax Deeds and Tax Liens.

When an investor purchases Tax Deeds the investor is actually purchasing the parcel at the auction.

A tax deed sale occurs only after homeowners fail to pay property taxes, but how the process works depends on the state the property is located in.

In every state that allows these sales, a government body – usually the county in which the home sits – must first get a tax deed. This is the legal document that gives the government body the right to sell a home to collect the delinquent taxes it's owed.
Once the government agency has its tax deed, it can put the home up for sale during a public auction. The county will usually set a minimum bid for the homes it is selling. Buyers then bid on the properties and the highest bidder wins. At a deed sale the property owner has no chance of getting the property back (redeeming) unless it is a redeemable deed state.

Tax Liens
Tax Liens are a little more complicated to explain because you are not purchasing a parcel you are purchasing the lien on a parcel that is issued though a certificate, called a tax lien certificate. If the owner does not pay their property taxes plus any interest or penalties due then the investor will get the parcel debt free in most cases. We will talk about the exceptions to the property being debt free in another teaching.

Web Site: https://befreeuniversity.com **Phone:** 855.5BE.FREE

There are 6 Steps to Acquiring a Tax Lien Property

1. The Local Municipality Creates A Tax Lien Certificate

Local governments charge property taxes to help fund government programs and services. If a homeowner fails to pay their property tax bill, the local government places a lien and creates a tax lien certificate. This certificate includes information such as the amount of tax due, as well as any interest or penalties. If the property owner still doesn't pay their tax bill (with interest), then the government has the right to foreclose on the home.

2. The Tax Lien Certificate Is Put Up for Auction

In 28 states, the government can sell tax lien certificates to private investors, which allows them to recoup their losses more quickly. This sale usually happens at a tax lien auction, where the certificate goes to the best bidder. Every county in the country has a tax auction at least once a year, unless circumstances do not allow (such as the pandemic).

3. Investors Bid On The Tax Lien Certificate

Depending on the auction, bids may be based on either the cash amount someone is willing to pay for the certificate or the interest rate they're willing to accept. In the case of cash offers, a certificate goes to the highest bidder. In the case of interest rate, it goes to the lowest bidder.

Keep in mind that the lower the interest rate you bid on a tax lien certificate, the lower the profit you could potentially receive. Bidding wars on tax liens can drive the interest rate – and therefore the profit – down. There are a few states that utilize the bidding down of interest rates.

4. Winning Investor Takes Control Of the Property

The winning bidder of a tax lien auction takes ownership of the tax lien certificate. This doesn't technically give them ownership of the property. But it gives them the right to take ownership of the property through foreclosure or be paid back when the homeowner eventually pays their tax bill.

5. Investor Pays the Amount of Taxes Owed

 BE FREE
UNIVERSITY

Web Site: https://befreeuniversity.com **Phone:** 855.5BE.FREE

When you win a tax lien auction, you're immediately responsible for paying the tax bill, including any interest or fees owed. Then, the homeowner has a certain period of time before the redemption period deadline, by which time they must pay the new investor or risk foreclosure.

6. Repayment or Foreclosure

When you purchase a tax lien certificate, there are two potential outcomes: either the homeowner will pay their property taxes, or they won't. If the homeowner pays their property taxes, then you make back your initial investment, plus the interest rate determined by state law or at the auction.

If the homeowner doesn't pay their property taxes, then you have the right to begin the foreclosure process. Depending on the state, there may be an expiration date, which requires you to initiate foreclosure within a certain amount of time after buying the tax lien. This process varies by state and county. In some counties the foreclosure process is done by the county and in other the county leaves it up to you. Either way, you have the ability to obtain property inexpensively.

In this program the Tax Lien Master we discuss Tax Liens and Deeds in detail as my team walk you through an entire process of how to successfully get a tax lien or deed and even the strategy on how to get a property an average of 80% of the time when the steps are applied correctly.

In this special guide, I want to walk you through each state, introduce what their investment rates are, how they work (Tax Lien, Deed, Hybrid), and how that can completely change you and your financial career.

I want to preface with this - I'm not superman and I don't have the ability to fly places fast, so there are counties and states I haven't spent as much time in as others, and things change, so don't hold it against me if you find an error.

This is why technology can help us master Liens and Deeds. You can pick up the phone, and literally use wires throughout the sky to speak to someone who can tell you exactly how the counties work, and how they run their Tax Auctions. (And receive updates on aspects of Tax Sales that are shifting.)

Remember, it is ALWAYS a good idea to double check your counties procedure when it comes to Tax Auctions, there is nothing worse than getting to auction and finding out you needed to register before 8 Am, or the day before. I've done it before, and I don't want you making the same COSTLY mistake as me.

I will also say - This IS NOT an Ultimate guide that will be the only thing you ever need to invest in Tax Liens, but it is an INCREDIBLE start. I'm going to give you the information that most people HATE getting themselves, and it will save you hours of researching government websites trying to find information.

If you use this tool correctly, you will find yourself saving a lot of time trying to figure out which counties will be best for your investment strategy. And if you couple this with my Tax Lien Master Program (Which I'll offer you a great discount at the end), you'll soar through your learning phase and have the skills and tools to dive right into actually making money in Real Estate Investing.

I hope this guide helps you in the ways it has helped me,

Financial Moses
Be Free University
www.befreeuniversit.com

Tax Deeds

Tax Deeds are a great way to get properties if you have an above average investing budget. That's not to say that you can find KILLER deals that will blow you away for cheap (Over the Counter Deeds), but as a general rule, in the bigger counties, investors will bid up the Tax Deed to almost full value.

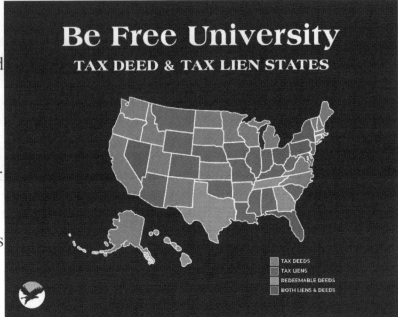

It is our job, as intelligent investors, to find the counties that aren't nearly as busy, and focus on those, to get quick properties, sell them quick, and continue the process, gaining cash flow, then being able to step up into the bigger counties and compete amongst the big leagues. (If that's something that interests you!)

REMEMBER: When you are purchasing a Tax Deed, it is important to understand that you are actually purchasing the *property*. You become the sole owner of that property; therefore, you are responsible to pay for the Taxes on the property. You are also responsible for back liens, (unless the state rules clear out all liens, which is common, but you MUST check first.)

Keep this in mind when bidding. It can reward you with great returns, but you must do your due diligence and understand the process and how each county that you want to be investing in works.

Tax Deed State List

Alaska	Michigan	North Dakota
Arkansas	Minnesota	Ohio
California		Oklahoma
Idaho	Nevada	Oregon
Kansas	New Mexico	Utah
Maine	New York	Virginia
Massachusetts	North Carolina	Washington
		Wisconsin

Alaska

In this Tax Deed State auctions start at Tax Accessor Appraised value. Alaska uses the seal bid process (you can learn more about this process in the Tax Lien and Deed Master Class".) The OTC (Over the Counter) process is used for the parcels that are left over and do not sell.

This state will actually issue a warranty deed as opposed to a tax deed which should avert the quiet title process because you have clear title. However, each Title Company may view the deed process differently.

REMEMBER: You should never purchase a property site unseen. We will discuss this more in the Tax Lien and Deed Master Class.

Summary: Unless a local ordinance provides otherwise, delinquent real property taxes must be collected through the annual foreclosure proceedings (Sec. 29.45.320,

Sec. 29.45.360). Foreclosed properties are transferred to the municipality (Sec. 29.45.390) for the lien amount, which must retain the properties for at least a one (1) year redemption period (Sec. 29.45.400). Unredeemed property in the area of the borough outside all cities is deeded to the borough by the clerk of the court (Sec. 29.45.450). Unredeemed property in a city is deeded to the city subject to the payment by the city of unpaid borough taxes and costs of foreclosure levied against the property before foreclosure. After that, the local city or borough has the option of retaining the property for public use or selling it (Sec. 29.45.460).

Law: Alaska Statutes, Title 29, Chapter 45, Article 2, u201cEnforcement of Tax Liens.u201d

Contact: Municipal clerk or designee (Sec. 29.45.460 (c)).

Interest Rate: Not applicable.

Auction Type: Tax Deed (Sec. 29.45.460 (b)).

Bidding Procedure: Premium bid / highest bid. (Sec. Sec. 29.45.480).
Costs: Not specified by statute.

Redemption Period: Not applicable.

Deed Assigned at Foreclosure to: The city or borough (Sec. 29.45.460).

u201c (a) Unredeemed property in the area of the borough outside all cities is deeded to the borough by the clerk of the court. Unredeemed property in a city is deeded to the city subject to the payment by the city of unpaidu00a0borough taxes and costs of foreclosure levied against the property before foreclosure. The deed shall beu00a0recorded in the recording district in which the property is located.

(b) Conveyance gives the municipality clear title, except for prior recorded tax liens of the United States and the state.

(c) If unredeemed property lies in a city and if the city has no immediate public use for the property but the borough does have an immediate public use, the city shall deed the property to the borough. If unredeemed property lies in the borough outside all cities and if the borough does not have an immediate public use for the property but a city does have an immediate public use, the borough shall deed the property to the city.

(d) A deed is not invalid for irregularities, omissions, or defects in the proceedings under this chapter unless the former owner has been misled so as to be injured. Two years after the date of the deed, its validity is conclusively presumed and a claim of

BE FREE UNIVERSITY

Web Site: https://befreeuniversity.com **Phone:** 855.5BE.FREE

the former owner or other person having an interest in the property
is forever barred. The municipality or borough may then sell the property if it is not
required for a public purpose. u201d

Arkansas

Info for Arkansas: This state grants the deed at the sale however the homeowner
will receive a 30-day redemption period in which they are responsible for the
taxes, interest and penalty however the penalties and interest is not awarded to the
Tax Deed Investor.

Summary: (a)(1) All lands upon which the taxes have not been paid for one (1)
year following the date the taxes were due, October 10, shall be forfeited to the
State of Arkansas and transmitted by certification to the Commissioner of State
Lands for collection or sale. (Sec. 26-37-101), who may sell the property at a
public auction following a two-year redemption period (Sec. 26-37-301).

Law: Arkansas Code of 1987, Title 26, Chapter 37, "Sale or Forfeiture of Real
Property." Contact: County Tax Collectors or Commissioner of State Lands (Sec.
26-37-203). Interest Rate: Not applicable.

Auction Type: Tax Deed (Sec. 26-37-202 (e) (3)). "If the land is not redeemed, a
limited warranty deed will be issued by the Commissioner of State Lands to the
purchaser."

Bidding Procedure: Premium bid / highest bid. (Sec. 26-37-201). "The highest
bidder shall pay all taxes, interest, penalties, and other costs."

According to (Sec. 26-37-302), "(a) Bidders may bid at the sale or mail their bid to
the office of the Commissioner of State Lands. Bids shall be delivered at the
appropriate place before the deadline established in the notice of sale.
(b) If no one bids at least the assessed value, the Commissioner may negotiate a
sale. All negotiated sales shall have approval of the Attorney General of the State
of Arkansas.
(c) The Commissioner shall conduct tax-delinquent sales in the county wherein the
land is located, unless the Commissioner determines that there are not enough

parcels of land to justify a sale in one (1) county only. In that case, the Commissioner may hold a tax-delinquent land sale in one (1) location and thereat sell land located in more than one (1) county if the counties wherein the lands are located are adjoining counties.

(d) The sales shall be conducted on the dates specified in the notices required by this subchapter.

(e) (1) After a sale of the land by the Commissioner of State Lands, including a negotiated sale, the Commissioner of State Lands shall notify the owner and all interested parties of the right to redeem the land within thirty (30) days after the date of the sale paying all taxes, penalties, interest, and costs due, including the cost of the notice.

(2) The notice under subdivision (e)(1) of this section shall be sent by regular mail to the last known address of the owner and all interested parties.

(3) If the land is not redeemed, a limited warranty deed will be issued by the Commissioner of State

Lands to the purchaser."

Costs: Fees and costs payable by a purchaser at a tax sale include all costs of notices (Sec. 26-37-104) and

The Commissioner of State Lands shall charge a twenty-five-dollar ($25.00) collection fee for each deed issued by the Commissioner of State Lands, whether the land is redeemed or sold. (Sec. 26-37-105). The public notice shall contain the amount of taxes, interest, penalties, and other costs due on the land; (Sec. 26-37-201).

Redemption Period: Thirty-days (30) (Sec. 26-37-202). An owner or other interested party may redeem tax- delinquent land at any time up until the tax sale (Sec. 26-37-301), as well as during the 30 days following the date of the sale (Sec. 26-37-202). A special redemption period applies for persons under disability, who have two years from the expiration of their disability to redeem their property (Sec. 26-37-305).

Deed Assigned at Foreclosure to: The purchaser (Sec. 26-37-203). "(a) If the tax-delinquent land is not redeemed within the thirty-day period, the Commissioner of State Lands shall issue a limited warranty deed to the land."

Web Site: https://befreeuniversity.com **Phone:** 855.5BE.FREE

Notes: Ninety (90) days after a public auction, parcels offered, but not sold, are available for sale through the Commissioner of State Lands office. You may request a list of properties available for a specific county by writing to the Commissioner of State Lands or by calling the Real Estate Division at 501-324-9422. The cost is fifty cents ($.50) per page. You will be invoiced for the list when it is mailed to you. The lists are now available on our website at www.cosl.org/ Please click on the "Publications" menu for easy access. The lists are updated daily.

According to (Sec. 26-37-201), the minimum bid not only includes taxes, interest, penalties, and other costs but the bid must also be equal to at least the assessed value of the land as certified to the Commissioner of State Lands.

California

Info for California: This state will usually take large amounts of capital due to the competitiveness and the high values of properties when compared to other states.

Note: If you would like to get started, I would not recommend starting in larger cities instead try starting in counties on the outside of the larger cities.

You will find some counties utilize online auctions. You can find more information about this at www.bid4assets.com.

Summary: According to (Sec. 3691) "(a) Annually, on or before June 8, the tax collector shall publish a notice of impending default for failure to pay taxes on real property, except tax-defaulted property and possessory interests, the taxes, assessments, penalties, and costs on which will have not been fully paid by the close of business on the last business day of the fiscal year. Five years or more after the property has become tax defaulted, the tax collector shall have the power to sell and shall attempt to sell in accordance with Section 3692 all or any portion of tax - defaulted property that has not been redeemed."

Law: California Revenue and Taxation Code, Division 1, Part 6, "Tax Sales," Part 7,

"Redemption," and Part 7.5, "Tax Certificates."
Contact: County Tax Collector/Treasurer (Sec. 3371).
Interest Rate: Not applicable.
Auction Type: Tax Deed (Sec. 3708).

"On receiving the full purchase price at any sale under this chapter, the tax collector shall, without charge, execute a deed to the purchaser."

Bidding Procedure: Premium bid / highest bid. (Sec. 3693). The basic procedures for conducting sales of tax certificates are established by local tax collectors (Sec. 4528). Unredeemed tax-defaulted property is sold to the highest bidder (Sec. 3693), subject to a minimum price requirement (Sec. 3698.5). If there are no acceptable bids at the attempted sale, the tax collector shall attempt to sell the property at intervals of no more than six years until the property is sold (Sec. 3692).

Costs: A long list of fees can be found in (Sec. 3698.5).
Redemption Period: Not applicable.

Deed Assigned at Foreclosure to: The purchaser (Sec. 3708). "On receiving the full purchase price at any sale under this chapter, the tax collector shall, without charge, execute a deed to the purchaser."

Recording the deed (Sec. 3708.1). "Upon execution the tax collector shall immediately record the deed with the county recorder and pay the recording fees. Recording of the deed shall constitute delivery thereof to the grantee named in the deed."

Idaho

Info for Idaho: In Idaho you will receive a deed at the sale however the auctions are not like other states. Most counties will sell to buyers who are interested in the properties. It may do you some good if you want to invest in this state to get to know those who are involved in the Tax Deed process.

Web Site: https://befreeuniversity.com **Phone:** 855.5BE.FREE

Statute Summary: (1) If real property on which there is a delinquency is not redeemed within three (3) years from the date of delinquency, the county tax collector of the county wherein such property is situated must make, in favor of said county, a tax deed for such property (Sec. 63-1005) The deed conveys to the grantee the absolute title to the land described therein, free of all encumbrances except mortgages of record to the holders of which notice has not been sent as provided in section 63-1005, Idaho Code, any lien for property taxes which may have attached subsequently to the assessment and any lien for special assessments.(Sec. 63-1009). Such property may be sold at public auction to the highest bidder (Sec. 31-808). Should the county be unable to sell at a public auction any real or personal property belonging to the county, including property acquired by tax deed, it may sell the property without further notice by public or private sale upon such terms and conditions as the county deems necessary. Distribution of the proceeds of sale shall be as set forth in subsection (2) of this section.

Law: Idaho Code, Title 31, Chapter 8, "Powers and Duties of Board of Commissioners," and Title 63, Chapter 10, "Collection of Delinquency on Real, Personal, and Operating Property."

Contact: County Tax Collectors (Sec. 63-1002).
Interest Rate: Not applicable.
Auction Type: Tax Deed (Sec. 31-808, Sec. 63-1011).

Bidding Procedure: Premium bid / highest bid. (Sec. 31-808). "The property shall be sold to the highest bidder. However, the board of county commissioners may reserve the right to reject any and all bids and shall have discretionary authority to reject or accept any bid which may be made for an amount less than the total amount of all delinquent taxes, late charges, costs and interest which may have accrued against any property so offered for sale, including the amount specified in the tax deed to the county."

Costs: According to (Sec. 31-808), "In addition to the purchase price, a purchaser of county property, including property acquired by tax deed, shall pay all fees required by law for the transfer of property. No deed for any real estate purchased pursuant to the provisions of this section shall be delivered to a purchaser until such deed has been recorded in the county making the sale."

 **BE FREE** UNIVERSITY   **Web Site:** https://befreeuniversity.com   **Phone:** 855.5BE.FREE

Redemption Period: Not applicable (Sec. 63-1007). "After the issuance of a tax deed, real property may be redeemed only by the record owner or owners, or party in interest, up to the time the county commissioners have entered into a contract of sale or the property has been transferred by county deed."

Deed Assigned at Foreclosure to: The purchaser (Sec. 63-1006). "If the county commissioners shall find that the county tax collector has conformed to the requirements of section 63-1005, Idaho Code, and that a delinquency was owing on the property described and that such delinquency has not been paid, the county commissioners shall immediately direct the county tax collector to issue a tax deed in favor of the county."

Kansas

Info for Kansas: Kanas is a deed state where the bidding will usually start fairly low compare to the actual property value. However, be careful as pricing can be bid up fairly easily because of competition.

Statute Summary: All real estate on which the taxes shall not have been paid as provided by law on or before the twentieth day of June in each year, commencing with the year 1941, shall be subject to sale as hereinafter provided. (Sec. 79-2301) If any county treasurer shall unavoidably omit or fail to sell any real estate for unpaid taxes on the first Tuesday of September, he or she shall advertise and sell such real estate on the fourth Monday of October next ensuing, and such advertisement and sale shall conform in all respects to the provisions of this act, and shall be as binding and valid as if such sale had been made on the first Tuesday of September. If any real estate on which the taxes shall not have been paid has been advertised as provided by law, and has not been sold to the county by reason of any injunction or judicial proceeding, after such injunction shall have been dissolved it shall only be necessary for the county treasurer to cause to be published in some newspaper of general circulation in his or her county a notice stating that such real estate was not sold, by reason of such injunction; and such real estate shall be sold to the county at such time and place as shall therein be specified, which time shall not be less than ten days from the date of publication, said sale to be conducted in the same manner as herein provided for the sale of other real estate for delinquent taxes (Sec. 79-2322). The county continues to hold the property during a two-year

redemption period (Sec. 79-2401a), after which the county may initiate a judicial foreclosure (Sec. 79-2801) which will eventually lead to the sale of the property at a public auction (Sec. 79-2804).

Law: Kansas Statutes, Chapter 79, Article 23, "Sale of Real Estate for Taxes," Article 24, "Redemption of Real Estate," and Article 28, "Judicial Foreclosure and Sale of Real Estate by County."

Contact: County Treasurers/Tax Collectors (Sec. 79-2804).

Interest Rate: Not applicable.

Auction Type: Tax Deed (Sec. 79-2804). Unredeemed property is sold at a public auction by the appointed county clerk to the highest bidder (Sec. 79-2804).

Bidding Procedure: Premium bid / highest bid. (Sec. 79-2804). "On the day fixed for the sale by such notice, the sheriff shall offer each such tract, lot or piece of real estate for sale, separately, and the same shall be sold at public auction for the highest and best bid obtainable."

Costs: Not specified by the state statutes. Contact county officials for details.

Redemption Period: Not applicable.

Deed Assigned at Foreclosure to: The sheriff shall make return to the clerk and the same, as soon as practicable, shall be examined by the court, and if found by the court to be regular, it shall be confirmed, and the sheriff ordered to forthwith execute to the purchasers at such sale a good and sufficient deed. (Sec. 79-2804 emphasis added).

Maine

Info for Maine: Maine is a Deed State and the process here is questionable as if you do not pay at least the back taxes on the property you may only receive a fractionable part of the parcel.

Statute Summary: A tax collector or constable of the municipality who shall have the same powers as the tax collector, may sell at auction real property on which taxes are delinquent (Sec. 1071). If any tax on real estate remains unpaid on the first Monday in February next after said tax was assessed, the tax collector shall sell at

public auction so much of such real estate as is necessary for the payment of said tax, interest and all the charges, at 9 o'clock in the forenoon of said first Monday in February at the office of the tax collector or at the place where the last preceding annual municipal meeting was held. When no person appears to discharge the taxes duly assessed on any such real estate of resident or nonresident owners, with costs of advertising, on or before the time of sale, the tax collector shall proceed to sell at public auction, to the highest bidder, so much of such real estate as is necessary to pay the tax due (Sec. 1071, Sec. 1074). The treasurer shall not at that time deliver the deeds to the grantees (purchaser), but put them on file in his office, to be delivered at the expiration of 2 years from the day of sale, and the treasurer shall after the expiration of 2 years deliver said deed to the grantee or his heirs, provided the owner, the mortgagee or any person in possession or other person legally taxable therefore does not within such time redeem the estate from such sale, by payment or tender of the taxes, all the charges and interest on the whole at the rate of 8% a year from the date of sale to the time of redemption, and costs as provided, with 67¢ for the deed and certificate of acknowledgment (Sec. 1076).

Law: Maine Revised Statutes, Title 36, Part 2, Chapter 105, Subchapter IX, "Delinquent Taxes."
Contact: Local tax collectors/constables (Sec. 1071).
Interest Rate: Not applicable.

Auction Type: Tax Deed (Sec. 1071). "If any tax on real estate remains unpaid on the first Monday in February next after said tax was assessed, the tax collector shall sell at public auction so much of such real estate as is necessary for the payment of said tax, interest and all the charges, at 9 o'clock in the forenoon of said first Monday in February at the office of the tax collector or at the place where the last preceding annual municipal meeting was held. In case of the absence or disability of the tax collector, the sale shall be made by some constable of the municipality who shall have the same powers as the tax collector."

Bidding Procedure: Premium bid / highest bid. (Sec. 1074). "The tax collector shall proceed to sell at public auction, to the highest bidder, so much of such real estate as is necessary to pay the tax due, in the case of each person assessed, If the bidding is for less than the whole, it shall be for a fractional part of the estate, and the bidder who will pay the sum due for the least fractional part shall be the purchaser."

BE FREE UNIVERSITY

Web Site: https://befreeuniversity.com **Phone:** 855.5BE.FREE

Costs: Statutory costs payable by a purchaser at a tax sale include $3 for advertising and sales costs, 25 cents for each copy and return required to be filed, 67 cents for the deed and certificate of acknowledgement, and an unspecified amount for printing costs (Sec. 1074).

Redemption Period: Not applicable.

 BE FREE UNIVERSITY

Web Site: https://befreeuniversity.com   **Phone:** 855.5BE.FREE

Massachusetts

Info for Massachusetts: Has both tax lien and tax deed certificate sale but most municipalities have tax deed certificate sales. 16% interest rate but there is no right of redemption after a tax deed sale.

Statute Summary: The collector shall give notice by publication of the time and place of sale of land for nonpayment of taxes (Chapter 60 Sec. 40), If the taxes are not paid, the collector shall, at the time and place appointed for the sale, sell by public auction the property for which taxes are delinquent (Sec. 43). If at the time and place of sale no person bids for the land offered for sale an amount equal to the tax and charges, and if the sale has been adjourned one or more times, the collector shall then and there make public declaration of the fact; and, if no bid equal to the tax and charges is then made, he shall give public notice that he purchases for the town by which the tax is assessed said land as offered for sale at the amount of the tax and the charges and expenses of the levy and sale. Said amount, together with the cost of recording the deed of purchase, shall be allowed him in his settlement with such town, provided he has caused the deed to be duly recorded within sixty days after the purchase and to be delivered to the town treasurer (Sec. 48). The collector shall execute and deliver to the purchaser a deed of the land. The deed shall convey the land to the purchaser, subject to the right of redemption. No sale hereafter made shall give to the purchaser any right to possession of the land until the right of redemption is foreclosed, as hereinafter provided (Sec. 45).

Law: Massachusetts General Laws, Chapter 60, "Collection of Local Taxes." Contact: Local tax collector (Chapter 60: Sec. 2, Sec. 43). Interest Rate: 16% per annum. (Chapter 60: Sec. 62) Auction Type: Hybrid Tax Deed (Sec. 45).

Bidding Procedure: Premium bid / highest bid. (Chap. 60 Sec. 43). "Bidder raises the amount payable above the minimum. The sale covers the smallest undivided part of the land which will bring said amount, or the whole for said amount. and shall at such sale require of the purchaser an immediate deposit of such sum as he considers necessary to ensure good faith in payment of the purchase money, and, on failure of the purchaser to make such deposit forthwith, the sale shall be void and another sale may be made."

Costs: Please see statute for a long list of costs & fess payable by the purchaser (Chapter 60: Sec. 15).

 BE FREE UNIVERSITY

Web Site: https://befreeuniversity.com **Phone:** 855.5BE.FREE

Redemption Period: Six (6) months (Chap. 60 Sec. 65). Any person having an interest in land taken or sold for nonpayment of taxes, may redeem the same by paying or tendering to the treasurer the amount of the tax title account of the land being redeemed, and interest at sixteen per cent upon the original sum for which the land was taken or sold, from the date of sale, and upon each sum certified, from the date of certification, together with all charges lawfully added to the tax title account of such land subsequently to such taking or sale, or may redeem the same by paying or tendering to said treasurer installments on account of the tax title account, each of which except the last, together with the full amount of interest, as aforesaid, to the date of payment of the amount of the tax title account or balance thereof remaining due at the time of such payment, and all charges lawfully added as aforesaid until the full amount of the tax title account, with interest as aforesaid and all such charges, is paid. (Sec. 62). The petition for foreclosure may be filed after six months from the date of the tax sale (Sec. 65).

Michigan

Info for Michigan: This Deed State has no redemption period for the homeowner. Meaning the investor is guaranteed the homeowner cannot redeem the property after the Deed Sale has occurred. This state has had several properties to sell for as little as $500.

You can find the state website at www.tax-sale.info. Nothing too fancy, but you'll be able to see which counties have parcels available.

Statute Summary: On March 1 in each tax year, certified abandoned property and property that is delinquent for taxes, interest, penalties, and fees for the immediately preceding 12 months or more is forfeited to the county treasurer for the total amount of those unpaid delinquent taxes, interest, penalties, and fees. (Sec.211.78a, Sec. 211.78g). The Tax Collector enters judgment on a petition for foreclosure filed under section 78h not more than 10 days after March 1 immediately succeeding the date the petition for foreclosure is filed for uncontested cases or 10 days after the conclusion of the hearing for contested cases. All redemption rights to the property expire 21 days after the circuit court enters a judgment foreclosing the property as requested in the petition for foreclosure. beginning on the third Tuesday in July

BE FREE UNIVERSITY

Web Site: https://befreeuniversity.com **Phone:** 855.5BE.FREE

immediately succeeding the entry of the judgment under section 78k vesting absolute title to tax delinquent property in the foreclosing governmental unit, the foreclosing governmental unit, or its authorized representative, at the option of the foreclosing governmental unit, may hold 1 or more property sales at 1 or more convenient locations at which property foreclosed by the judgment entered under section 78k shall be sold by auction sale. (Sec. 211.78m). If the property is not sold, then beginning on the third Tuesday in September all property not previously sold by the foreclosing governmental shall be offered or reoffered for sale, subject to the same requirements set forth in subsection.

Beginning on the third Tuesday in November, all property not previously sold shall again be reoffered for sale, except that the minimum bid shall not be required.

Law: Michigan Compiled Laws, Chapter 211, Sec. 211.60 et seq., "Sale, Redemption, and Conveyance of Delinquent Tax Lands."
Contact: County treasurer (Sec. 211.78m).
Interest Rate: Not applicable under the current collection system because there is no right to redeem foreclosed property sold at a tax sale.
Auction Type: Tax Deed (Sec. 211.78m).
Bidding Procedure: Premium bid / highest bid. (Sec. 211.78m (2)). Property shall be sold to the person bidding the highest amount above the minimum bid. The foreclosing governmental unit may require full payment by cash, certified check, or money order at the close of each day's bidding (Sec. 211.78m).

Costs: The minimum bid amount includes all expenses of administering the sale, including all preparations for the sale paid in full at the close of each day's bidding (Sec. 211.78m).
Redemption Period: Not applicable; the deed shall vest fee simple title to the property in the person bidding the highest amount above the minimum bid (Sec. 211.78m).
Deed Assigned at Foreclosure to: Tax Deed sale purchaser (Sec. 211.78m).

Minnesota

Info for Minnesota: This Deed State will allow counties to finance properties, deed will only be granted when the financing is paid in full. The bid will begin at

the counties appraised property value plus 3%.

Statute Summary: Real estate for which property taxes have been determined delinquent are "sold" to the state in May of each year (Sec. 280.43, Sec. 280.001). If the real property is not redeemed, it then becomes tax-forfeited land (Sec. 281.23). The county auditor shall then offer the parcels of land in order in which they appear in the notice of sale, and shall sell them to the highest bidder, but not for a sum less than the appraised value, until all of the parcels of land have been offered (Sec. 282.01 Subd. **7).**

Law: Minnesota Statutes, Chapter 280, "Real Estate Tax Judgment Sales," Chapter 281, "Real Estate Tax Sales, Redemption," and Chapter 282, "Tax- Forfeited Land Sales."

Contact: County auditors (Sec. 282.01).

Interest Rate: Not applicable.

Auction Type: Tax Deed (Sec. 282.301). "Upon payment in full of the purchase price, the purchaser or the assignee shall receive a warranty deed from the state, to be executed by the commissioner of revenue."

Bidding Procedure: Premium bid / highest bid. (Sec. 282.01). "Tax-forfeited land is sold to the highest bidder, but not for less than the appraised value of the land. A county board may provide for sales on terms."

Costs: General costs and fees are not specified by state statute (Sec. 282.261a)

Redemption Period: Not applicable.

Deed Assigned at Foreclosure to: The Purchaser at the tax sale subject to right to redeem (Sec. 282.01).

Nevada

Info for Nevada: This exciting state is not only known for its casinos but also for their awesome properties and values. Their tax deed sale will grant a clear title upon acquisition with the exception of Federal liens.

Summary: Property for which taxes are delinquent, are held by the county treasurer, subject to a two year right of redemption. (Sec. 361.5648, Sec. 361. 570).

If the property is not redeemed during that period, then under order by the board of county commissioners, the county treasurer can sell the property, after giving notice of sale, for a total amount not less than the amount of the taxes, costs, penalties and interest legally chargeable against the property as stated in the order. (Sec. 361.595).

Law: Nevada Revised Statutes, Chapter 361, "Property Tax."
Contact: County Treasurer. (Sec. 361.595)
Interest Rate: Not applicable.
Auction Type: Tax Deed. (Sec. 361.595 (4)).
Bidding Procedure: Premium bid / highest bid. (Sec. 361.595 (2)). Sale is to the highest bidder for not less than the amount of taxes, costs, penalties, and interest legally chargeable against the property as stated (Sec. 361.595 (2)).

Costs: Cost and fees payable by the purchaser, are not specified by the state statutes. (Sec. 361.595).
Redemption Period: Not applicable.
Deed Assigned at Foreclosure to: The winning bidder/purchaser at the public tax sale (Sec. 361.595). April 29th

New Mexico

Info for New Mexico: New Mexico conduct sales up to 4 times in a year and most counties use the premium bid process. The minimum bid must be greater than or equal to the total of all delinquent taxes, penalties, interests, and costs.

Most counties also use competitive bidding with a starting price that is similar to the taxes owed.

Owners of the property can challenge the sale for up to 2 years after purchase date.

Summary: By July 1 of each year, the county treasurer shall prepare a tax delinquency list of all real property for which taxes have been delinquent for more than two years. (Sec. 7-38-61). After the receipt of the tax delinquency list, the department has the responsibility and exclusive authority to take all action

BE FREE UNIVERSITY

Web Site: https://befreeuniversity.com **Phone:** 855.5BE.FREE

necessary to collect delinquent taxes shown on the list. (Sec. 7-38-62). Real property may then be sold for delinquent taxes after the expiration of three years from the first date shown on the tax delinquency list on which the taxes on the real property became delinquent. (Sec. 7-38-65, Sec. 7-38-67).

Law: New Mexico Statutes, Chapter 7, Article 38, "Administration and Enforcement of Property **Taxes.**"
Contact: County Assessor-Collector. (Sec. 7-38-62).
Interest Rate: Not applicable.
Auction Type: Tax Deed. (Sec. 7-38-70a). Upon receiving payment for real property sold for delinquent taxes, the division shall execute and deliver a deed to the purchaser. (Sec. 7-38-70a).

Bidding Procedure: Premium bid / highest bid. (Sec. 7-38-67). The property is sold to the highest bidder who offers at least the minimum price set by the Department (Sec. 7-38-67). The minimum price must not be less than the total of all delinquent taxes, penalties, interests, and costs.

Costs: Payment of delinquent taxes listed and any penalty, interest or costs due in connection with those taxes shall be made to the department if occurring after the receipt by the department of the tax delinquency list (Sec. 7-38-62). The notice of sale will specify the costs that are due (Sec. 7-38-66).
Redemption Period: Not applicable.

Deed Assigned at Foreclosure to: Upon receiving payment for real property sold for delinquent taxes, the division shall execute and deliver a deed to the purchaser. (Sec. 7-38-70).

Notes: According to (Sec. 7-1-49 New Window) when an investor purchase a property at a New Mexico Tax Deed Sale the investor takes it 'subject to all outstanding prior interests and encumbrances (i.e., mortgages) of record'.

New York

Info for New York: This state is mostly a deed state however you will find some counties that utilize the lien process. Tax Liens in the City of New York are not typically sold to the public. These special properties are mostly for companies that

have an agreement with the City of New York.

There are a few counties in New York that now have their sales online. You can find them at www.nysauctions.com.

Each county is different so make sure you study and do research based on the rules of each individual county. You will have access to each county name, number, population and contact information in our Tax Lien and Deed Masterclass.

Summary: Twenty-one months after lien date, or as soon thereafter as is practicable, the enforcing officer shall execute a petition of foreclosure pertaining to those properties which remain subject to delinquent tax liens (Sec. 1120, Sec. 1123). In the event of a failure to redeem or answer by any person having the right to redeem or answer, such person shall forever be barred and foreclosed of all right, title, and interest and equity of redemption in and to the parcel in which the person has an interest and a judgment in foreclosure may be taken by default as provided by subdivision three of section eleven hundred thirty-six of this title. (Sec.1123, Sec. 1131, Sec. 1136). Whenever any tax district shall become vested with the title to real property by virtue of a foreclosure proceeding brought pursuant to the provisions of this article, such tax district is hereby authorized to sell and convey the real property so acquired, either with or without advertising for bids, notwithstanding the provisions of any general, special or local law. (Sec. 1166).

Law: New York Real Property Tax Law, Chapter 50-a, Article 11, "Uniform Delinquent Tax Enforcement Act."
Contact: Local treasurer or the enforcing officer of each tax district (Sec. 1102, Sec. 1122).
Interest Rate: Not applicable
Auction Type: Tax Deed. (Sec. 1166 (1)). Whenever any tax district shall become vested with the title to real property by virtue of a foreclosure proceeding brought pursuant to the provisions of this article, such tax district is hereby authorized to sell and convey the real property so acquired, either with or without advertising for bids, (Sec. 1166). These types of sales require approval and confirmation by the district's governing body, except when the property is sold at public auction to the highest bidder.

Web Site: https://befreeuniversity.com **Phone:** 855.5BE.FREE

Bidding Procedure: Premium bid / highest bid. (Sec. 1102 (3)).

Costs: Not specified.

Redemption Period: The redemption period shall expire two years after lien date (Sec. 1110). A tax district may adopt a local law without referendum increasing the redemption period for residential or farm property, or both, to three or four years after lien date (Sec. 1111). As early as 6 months in New York City.

Deed Assigned at Foreclosure to: The Local Taxing district (Sec. 1131, Sec. 1136).

Notes: The city of New York holds an annual tax lien sale; the winning bidder will receive a tax lien certificate. Visit the following link to learn more http://www.nyc.gov/html/dof/html/property/property_bill_taxlien.shtml.

North Carolina

Info for North Carolina: This deed state has a process where a bid can be upset within 10 days of becoming the highest bid. This is known as an "upset bid". You can also purchase parcels directly from the county "Surplus Properties," by submitting a written offer to the county.

Summary: Sales of real property to collect delinquent real estate property taxes follow a taxing district suing to judicially foreclose a tax lien (Sec. 105-374, Sec. 105-375). State statute allows for two types of foreclosure proceedings, both result in the real estate being sold in fee simple, free and clear of all interests, rights, claims, and liens.

Law: General Statutes of North Carolina, Chapter 105, Subchapter II, Article 26, "Collection and Foreclosure of Taxes."

Contact: Local Tax Collectors (Sec. 105-350).

Interest Rate: Not applicable, because there is no right to redeem foreclosed property sold for delinquent real estate property taxes once the sale is confirmed (Sec. 105-374, Sec. 105-375).

Auction Type: Tax Deed (Sec. 105-374, Sec. 105-375).

Bidding Procedures: Premium bid / highest bid. (Sec. 105-374 (m). The sale shall be by public auction to the highest bidder at public auction for an amount equal to at

least the delinquent taxes, interest, penalties, and costs and shall, in accordance with the judgment, be held at the courthouse door on any day of the week except a Sunday or legal holiday (Sec. 105-374, Sec. 105-375).

Costs: Costs and fees payable by a winning purchaser of foreclosed property include the costs of the foreclosure proceeding, including reasonable attorney's fees and a commissioner's fee of not more than 5% of the purchase price (Sec. 105-374, Sec. 105-375). Redemption Period: There is no right of redemption on foreclosed property once the sale is confirmed (Sec.105-374, Sec. 105-375).

Deed Assigned at Foreclosure to: The tax deed sale purchaser (Sec. 105-374, Sec. 105-375).

Notes: According to 415 2111.12171.1 A 10-day period is provided by law for the filing of upset bids; if that ten 10-day period expires and no upset bids have been filed, the property is considered legally sold. Filing Upset Bids After a property is sold at public auction but before 10 day upset bidding period elapses, any interested party may file an upset bid with the Special Proceedings Division. To file an upset bid, the bid must be raised by at least 5% and either $50.00 or 5% of the new bid whichever is greater must be deposited with the clerk of the Superior Court. Once an upset bid is filed, a new ten day upset bidding period begins. Once this upset bidding period expires and no new upset bids have been filed, the property will be considered legally sold to the highest bidding party. If the highest bidding party defaults on their bid, they lost their deposit and a new sale process begins.

North Dakota

Info for North Dakota: The sales in this state are usually held on the third Tuesday in November. North Dakota also has an OTC sale however this differs county by county so take the initiative to request this information in each county you would like to participate.

Summary: Property on which real estate property taxes have been delinquent for four or more years Pass any interest of the owner, mortgagee, or lien holder in the

property to the county (Sec. 57-28-01, Sec. 57-28-08). After the date of foreclosure for property with an unsatisfied tax lien, the county auditor shall issue a tax deed to the county (Sec. 57-28-09), All property acquired by the county by tax deed must be appraised by the board of county commissioners at least thirty days before the annual sale under this chapter. The appraised price must be sufficient to cover all taxes, special assessments, homestead credit for special assessments, penalties, interest, and costs which were due against the property at the time of the service of the notice of foreclosure of tax lien, plus an amount equal to the estimated taxes and special assessments for the current assessment year (Sec. 57-28-10) The annual sale of land acquired by tax deed must be held at the county auditor's office or the usual place of holding district court in the county beginning on the third Tuesday of November of each year (Sec. 57-28-13, Sec. 57-28-15). Any property not sold at the annual November sale may be sold by the county auditor at private sale before the next annual November sale for not less than the property's minimum sale price. (Sec. 57-28-17).

Law: North Dakota Century Code, Title 57, Chapter 57-28, "Rights of County When Lands Not Redeemed."

Contact: County Treasurer or County Auditor. (Sec. 57-28-15).
Interest Rate: Not applicable.
Auction Type: Tax Deed (Sec. 57-28-16).
Bidding Procedure: Premium bid / highest bid. (Sec. 57-28-15). "Each parcel of land must be sold at auction to the highest bidder for no less than the minimum sale price as fixed before the sale. The sale may be made either for cash or one-fourth of the purchase price in cash, and the balance in equal annual installments over a period of not more than ten years. The purchaser may pay any or all annual installments with interest before the agreed due date of the installments. 2. If the sale is for cash, the purchaser shall promptly pay the amount bid to the county treasurer. 3. If the purchase price is to be paid in installments, the purchaser shall pay the first installment to the county treasurer and be given a contract for deed setting forth the terms of the sale. The contract for deed must be executed by the purchaser, the chairman of the board of county commissioners, and the county auditor. The contract must be in a form prescribed by the state tax commissioner. The contract must give the county the right to cancel the contract by resolution and due notice upon default by the purchaser."

Costs: not specified by the state statutes.
Redemption Period: There is no right to redeem forfeited property that has been

sold to at auction to a private purchaser (Sec. 57-28-19).

Deed Assigned at Foreclosure to: The purchaser at the delinquent property tax sale (Sec. 57-28-16).

Ohio

Info for Ohio: This state is one that can be confusing. Some counties are lien state and some counties are deed state however some counties only sell in parcels in bulk. Selling in bulk means the investor may need a large sum of funding to buy properties in bulk. Each county should also be contacted individually as some counties have OTC "Over the Counter" sales. We discuss OTC sales in the Tax Lien Master Class.

Summary: Generally, the court may order each parcel delinquent in property tax to be sold, without appraisal, for not less than either of the following: (1) The fair market value of the parcel, as determined by the county auditor, plus the costs incurred in the foreclosure proceeding;(2) The total amount of the finding entered by the court, including all taxes, assessments, charges, penalties, and interest (Sec. 5721.19). Every tract of land and town lot, that has been advertised and offered for sale on two separate occasions, not less than two weeks apart, and not sold for want of bidders, shall be forfeited to the state. (Sec. 5723.01) The county auditor shall maintain a list of forfeited lands and shall offer such lands for sale annually, or more frequently if the auditor determines that more frequent sales are necessary. (Sec. 5723.04).

Counties having a population of at least 200,000, may collect delinquent taxes by selling tax lien certificates at public auction (Sec. 5721.31). Upon the sale and delivery of a tax certificate, such tax certificate vests in the certificate holder the first lien previously held by the state and its taxing districts under section 5721.10 of the Revised Code for the amount of taxes, assessments, interest, and penalty charged against a certificate parcel,
superior to all other liens and encumbrances upon the parcel described in the tax certificate, in the amount of the certificate redemption price, except liens for delinquent taxes, assessments, penalties, interest, charges, and costs that attached to the certificate parcel prior to the attachment of the lien being conveyed by the sale of such tax certificate. (Sec. 5721.35). A county treasurer may, in the treasurer's discretion, negotiate the sale of any number of tax certificates with one

Web Site: https://befreeuniversity.com **Phone:** 855.5BE.FREE

or more persons, (Sec. 5721.33). Counties eligible to sell certificates include Butler, Cuyahoga, Franklin, Hamilton, Lake, Loraine, Lucas, Mahoning, Montgomery, Stark, Summit, and Trumbull counties.

Law: Ohio Revised Code, Title 57, Chapter 5721, "Delinquent Lands," and Chapter 5723, "Forfeited Lands."

Contact: The County Treasurer. (Sec. 5721.31). In all proceedings relating to delinquent and forfeited lands and the certification and sale thereof, the county auditor shall act as the agent of the state (Sec. 5721.09). The county treasurer shall compile a separate list, the list of parcels selected for tax certificate sales (Sec. 5721.31).

Interest Rate: Not applicable for tax deed sales (Sec. 5721.25). For sales of tax certificates, the maximum interest rate is 18% per annum simple interest (Sec. 5721.32 (C)).

Auction Type: Tax Deed Sale (Sec. 5721.19) or Tax Lien Certificate (Sec. 5721.31), depending on the county population and discretion.

Bidding Procedure: Premium bid / highest bid. (Sec. 5721.19). The county treasurer, designee, or agent shall award the tax certificate to the person bidding the lowest certificate rate of interest. (Sec. 5721.32). Bids are placed in even increments of one-fourth of one per cent to the rate of zero per cent.

Costs: Costs included in the minimum bid amount for sales of foreclosed property include amount of the taxes, assessments, charges, penalties, and interest, and the costs incurred in the foreclosure proceeding instituted against it, which are due and unpaid (Sec. 5721.19). The treasurer shall set the fee at a reasonable amount that covers the treasurer's costs of administering the sale of the tax certificate (Sec. 5721.32).

Redemption Period: There is no right to redeem foreclosed property (tax deeds) that is sold at a tax sale (Sec.5721.25). At any time prior to payment to the county treasurer by the certificate holder to initiate foreclosure proceedings under division (B) of section 5721.37 of the Revised Code, the owner of record of the certificate parcel, or any other person entitled to redeem that parcel, may redeem the parcel by paying to the county treasurer an amount equal to the total of the certificate redemption prices of all tax certificates respecting that parcel plus the sum of taxes, assessments, penalties, charges, and interest charged against the parcel that have become due and payable since the date the last certificate was sold (Sec. 5721.38). At any time after one year from the date shown on the tax certificate

Web Site: https://befreeuniversity.com **Phone:** 855.5BE.FREE

as the date the tax certificate was sold, and not later than three years after that date, the certificate holder may file with the county treasurer a request for foreclosure on a form prescribed by the tax commissioner and provided by the county treasurer (Sec. 5721.37).

Deed Assigned at Foreclosure to: Tax sale purchaser (Sec. 5721.19) or certificate holder (Sec. 5721.37), as applicable.

Notes: Tax Lien Certificate Sales: According to (Sec. 5721.31 New Window) 'Counties having a population of at least 200,000, may collect delinquent taxes by selling tax lien certificates at public auction'.

Oklahoma

Info for Oklahoma: This Deed State auctions are usually held on the Second Monday in June. The starting bid amount is usually 2/3 of the county assessed value of the property.

Summary: The county treasurer shall in all cases, except those provided for in subsection B of this section, where taxes are a lien upon real property and are unpaid on the first day of April of any year proceed, as hereinafter provided, to advertise and sell such real estate for such taxes, special assessments and costs, and shall not be bound before so doing to proceed to collect by sale all personal taxes on personal property which are by this Code made a lien on realty, but shall include such personal tax with that due on the realty, and shall sell the realty for all of said taxes and special assessments. (Sec. 3105). On the first Monday in October in each year between the hours of 9:00 a.m. and 4:00 p.m., the treasurer shall offer at public sale at his office whereby law the taxes are made payable, all lands, town lots or other real property which shall be liable for taxes of any description for the preceding year, or years, and which shall remain due and unpaid. (Sec. 3107), the first person who offers to pay the full amount due on any parcel of land shall be considered to be the successful purchaser.

BE FREE UNIVERSITY

Web Site: https://befreeuniversity.com **Phone:** 855.5BE.FREE

In the event a tax lien is not purchased at the tax lien certificate sale the (Sec. 3108). Property for which a minimum bid is not made is sold to the county. (68-3125) If any real estate purchased by the county at delinquent tax sale shall remain unredeemed for a period of two (2) years from date of sale, the county treasurer shall proceed to sell such real estate at resale, which shall be held on the second Monday of June each year in each county.

In the event a property is not purchased (68-3135) under the provisions of the resale tax laws may be sold by the county treasurer, after notice by publication, at a price as may be approved by the board of county commissioners, the notice to be given after receipt of bid on the property. (68-3135 B) The auctions shall be held at a time, date and place as set by the county treasurer with the approval of the county commissioners. On the date of the auction, the property or properties shall be sold by the county treasurer to the highest competitive bidder, for cash in hand. Any bid which is less than all of the real estate ad valorem taxes owed at the time of the original resale shall be accepted only upon approval of the county commissioners and the county excise board.

Law: Oklahoma Statutes, Title 68, Article 31, "Delinquent Taxes and Collection." Contact: The County Treasurer.
Interest Rate: 8% per annum. (Sec. 68-3113). More specifically, if the tax sale certificate is held by an individual purchaser, the sum paid to the county for such certificate and all taxes paid and endorsed thereon, together with interest thereon at the rate of eight percent (8%) per annum from the date of sale or purchase thereof from the county (Sec. 3113).
Auction Type: Tax Lien Certificate (68- 3111) and Tax Deed (68 –3135).
Bidding Procedures: Random selection or 'impartial drawing'. (Sec. 68-3108 (A)). The first person who offers to pay the full amount due on any parcel of land shall be considered to be the successful purchaser. In the event that more than one such person shall so appear at the same time the county treasurer shall decide the issue by fair and impartial drawing. Parcels of land shall be sold to prospective purchasers on a first-come,
first-served basis (Sec. 3108)

Costs: The county treasurer shall charge and collect, in addition to the taxes, interest and penalty, the publication fees as provided by the provisions of Section 121 of Title 28 of the Oklahoma Statutes, and Five Dollars ($5.00) plus postage for mailing the notice by certified mail, which shall be paid into the county treasury, and the county shall pay the cost of the publication of such notice and (Sec. 3106),

Web Site: https://befreeuniversity.com **Phone:** 855.5BE.FREE

the county treasurer shall collect an additional Ten Dollars ($10.00) for the issuance and acknowledgment of the certificate (Sec. 3111).

Redemption Period: Two (2) years. (Sec. 68-3117 (b)). The owner of any real estate sold for taxes, or any person having a legal or equitable interest therein, may redeem the same from the lien resulting from tax sale at any time before the execution of a deed of conveyance therefore by the county treasurer, by paying to the county treasurer, if the tax sale certificate is held by an individual purchaser, the sum paid to the county for such certificate and all taxes paid and endorsed thereon, together with interest thereon at the rate of eight percent (8%) per annum from the date of sale or purchase thereof from the county (Sec. 3113). If no person shall redeem any land on which the tax lien has been sold within two (2) years, at any time after the expiration, and on production of the certificate of purchase, the county treasurer of the county in which the sale of such land took place shall execute to the purchaser, or the heirs or assigns of the purchaser, a deed for land remaining unredeemed. A statute of limitation of seven (7) years is hereby fixed for tax sale certificates. No firm, association, corporation or individual holding a tax sale certificate shall be entitled to have a tax deed issued thereon after seven (7) years shall have elapsed from the date of the issuance of said tax sale certificate. (Sec. 3117, Sec. 3118).

Deed Assigned at Foreclosure to: Tax Lien Certificate holder. More specifically, the deed shall vest in the grantee an absolute estate in fee simple in the lands, subject however, to all claims which the state may have on the lands for taxes or other liens or encumbrances and shall extinguish the rights of any mortgagee of record of the lands to whom notice was sent as provided for by law (Sec. 3118).

Notes: Multiple Tax Sales: As far as Oklahoma is concerned, at 8% per annum it doesn't provide the biggest rate of return. However, it does keep the competition down.

The Oklahoma tax sale process can be a bit confusing but I'll do my best to make sense of it. First you should know that Oklahoma has three tax sales;
• Tax Sale
• Resales and
• County Commissioners Sales

The "Tax Sale" is held each year on the first Monday in October (Sec. 68-3107). The winning bidder receives a tax lien certificate which draws interest at 8% per

annum subject to a 2-year redemption period.

Any tax lien not sold at the "Tax Sale" is assigned to the county and can be purchased over the counter any time prior to the expiration of the 2-year redemption period (Sec. 68-3108).

The "Resale" or second buying opportunity includes properties which remain unredeemed for a period of two years from the date of the sale…" (Sec. 68-3125) and occurs the second Monday of June each year. The winning bidder will receive a treasurers or tax deed. Any property not sold at the "Resale" will be struck off to the county.

The "County Commissioners Sale" or third buying opportunity includes properties not sold at either the "tax sale" or the "resale". At the county commissioner sale "Properties are sold by the treasurer at a price approved by the county commissioners" (Sec. 68-3135).

Oregon

Info for Oregon: This Deed State holds auction to the public usually one time a year. This is a Premium bidding state where 80% of the assessed taxed value must be met.

Summary: Real property within the state of Oregon is subject to foreclosure for delinquent taxes whenever three years have elapsed from the earliest date of delinquency of taxes levied and charged thereon (Sec.312.010, Sec. 312.060). The court shall order that the several properties, against which the judgment and decree is entered, shall be sold directly to the county for the respective amounts of taxes and interest for which
the properties severally are liable. (Sec. 312.100). The properties not redeemed within the two-year period prescribed by (ORS 312.120) shall be deeded to the county by the tax collector (Sec. 312.200, Sec. 312.270). At that point, the county may sell the property or retain it for public use, at its discretion. See (ORS 275.090) for a list of statute approved property uses (Sec. 275.090).
Law: Oregon Revised Statutes, Title 25, Chapter 275, "County Lands," and Title 29, Chapter, 311, "Collection of Property Taxes," and Chapter 312, "Foreclosure of Property Tax Liens."

Contact: Tax collector. (Sec. 29-311.005). As used in the tax laws of this state, "tax collector" means the person or officer who by law is charged with the duty of collecting taxes assessed upon real property, and includes a deputy. (Sec. 311.005, Sec. 311.055).
Interest Rate: Not applicable.
Auction Type: Tax Deed. (Sec. 29-312.270). When a county acquires real property by foreclosure for delinquent taxes, the conveyance vests in the county title to the property, free from all liens and encumbrances except assessments levied by a municipal corporation for local improvements to the property. (2) A private purchaser at resale of such property by the county acquires title free and clear of all assessments for local improvements levied by any municipal corporation. (Sec. 275.090, Sec. 312.270).

Bidding Procedure: Premium bid / highest bid. (Sec. 25-275.190). All sales made under ORS 275.110 to 275.250 shall be to the highest and best bidder for cash or, in the discretion of the county court, for not less than 10 percent of the purchase price

in cash, the remainder to be paid under written agreement with the purchaser in equal installments over a term not exceeding 20 years from the date of sale, all deferred payments to bear interest from the date of sale at a rate set by the county court, payable annually. In advertising for bids, the county shall state whether the sale will be made for cash or by installment agreement. If by installment agreement, the county shall also state the term and the rate of interest to which the county will agree (Sec.275.110, Sec. 275.190).

Costs: Costs and fees payable are not specified by the state statutes

Redemption Period: All rights of redemption, with respect to the real properties therein described, shall terminate on the execution of the deed to the county. (Sec. 312.200).

Deed Assigned at Foreclosure to: To the Tax Sale Purchaser. (Sec. 275.090, Sec. 312.270).

Utah

Info for Utah: This Tax Deed State take up to 5 years for a delinquent property to reach a tax sale. This allows for the deterioration of properties to be significant meaning more rehabilitation for the investor. Knowing how to analyze a property and the potential for profits will be needed in this state. We cover how to Analyze Any Property in the Tax Lien Master Class. This is where good research will help you, and bad research can bring you down.

Summary: If any property is not redeemed by March 15 following the lapse of four years from the date when the property tax became delinquent, the county treasurer shall immediately file a listing with the county auditor of all properties whose redemption period is expiring in the nearest forthcoming tax sale. The tax sale shall be conducted in May or June of the current year. (Sec. 59-2-1343, Sec. 59-2-1351). The minimum bid must be an amount sufficient to pay the taxes, penalties, interest, and administrative costs, for less than the entire parcel. (Sec. 59-2-1351.1). Any property offered for sale for which there is no purchaser shall be struck off to the county by the county auditor, (Sec. 59-2-1351.3). The tax sale terminates any and all rights of redemption (Sec. 59-2-1346).

Web Site: https://befreeuniversity.com **Phone:** 855.5BE.FREE

Law: Utah Code, Title 59, Chapter 2, Part 13, "Collection of Taxes." Contact: County Treasurer or County Auditor (Sec. 59-2-1351). Interest Rate: Not applicable. (Sec. 59-2-1346, Sec. 59-2-1351.1). Auction Type: Tax Deed (Sec. 59-2-1351.1).

Bidding Procedure: Premium bid / highest bid. (Sec. 59-2-1351.1). Subject to the minimum bid requirements. The highest bid amount for the entire parcel of property, however, a bid may not be accepted for an amount which is insufficient to pay the taxes, penalties, interest, and administrative costs; or (b) a bid in an amount sufficient to pay the taxes, penalties, interest, and administrative costs, for less than the entire parcel. (Sec. 59-2-1351.1).

Costs: The administrative costs that are included in the minimum bid include the fee for recording the deed;
other costs payable by the tax sale purchaser are not specified in state statute (Sec. 59-2-1351.1).

Redemption Period: Not applicable. (Sec. 59-2-1346).

Deed Assigned at Foreclosure to: The tax sale purchaser (Sec. 59-2-1351.1).

Virginia

Info for Virginia: This Tax Deed State will issue a warranty deed that is free and clear from all liens upon acquisition.

Summary: When any taxes on any real estate in a county, city or town are delinquent on December 31 following the second anniversary of the date on which such taxes have become due, or, in the case of real property upon which is situated any structure that has been condemned by the local building official pursuant to applicable law or ordinance, the first anniversary of the date on which such taxes have become due, or, in the case of real estate which is deemed abandoned as provided herein, and the taxes on any real estate are delinquent on December 31 following the third anniversary of the date on which such taxes have become due, such real estate may be sold for the purpose of collecting all delinquent taxes on such property. (Sec.58.1-3965). Any owner of the real estate described in any notice published pursuant to § 58.1-3965 or any bill in equity filed pursuant to this article, or his or their heirs, successors and assigns, shall have the right to redeem such real

estate prior to the date set for a judicial sale thereof by paying into court all taxes, penalties and interest due with respect to such real estate, together with all costs including costs of publication and a reasonable attorney's fee set by the court. Any person who has paid any taxes on such real estate shall have a lien thereon for any taxes paid, plus interest at the rate of six percent per year. The right to redeem is ended when the property is sold. (Sec. 58.1-3974).

Law: Code of Virginia, Title 58.1, Subtitle III, Chapter 39, Article 4, "Bill in Equity for Sale of Delinquent Tax Lands."
Contact: Treasurer or Tax Collector. (Sec. 58.1-3910).
Interest Rate: Not applicable. (Sec. 58.1-3965, Sec. 58.1-3974).
Auction Type: Tax Deed. (Sec. 58.1-3967).
Bidding Procedure: Premium bid / highest bid. (Sec. 58.1-3969). The opening bid at a Virginia tax sale is the back real property taxes, penalties, interest, reasonable attorneys' fees, costs and any liens chargeable thereon subject to court confirmation (Sec. 58.1-3967, Sec. 58.1-3969).
Costs: Cost and fees payable by the purchaser of property sold for delinquent taxes are not specified by Virginia state statutes.

Redemption Period: Not applicable. (Sec. 58.1-3974).
Deed Assigned at Foreclosure to: The title conveyed to the purchaser at the judicial sale shall be held to bar any disabilities of parties' defendant, and shall be free of all claims of any creditor, person, or entity, including those claims of beneficiaries under any deed of trust or mortgage, provided that notice was given and the creditor, person, or entity was made a party defendant. (Sec. 58.1-3967).

Washington

Info for Washington: This Tax Deed State allows homeowners to be delinquent of property taxes for at least 3 years. This auction minimum bid is the amount of taxes, interest, and costs. Some of counties in this state are online and can be found on www.bid4assets.com.

Web Site: https://befreeuniversity.com **Phone:** 855.5BE.FREE

Summary: Once real estate has been delinquent in property taxes for at least three years the county treasurer may initiate foreclosure proceedings (Sec. 84.64.050). The county treasurer shall immediately after receiving the order and judgment of the court proceed to sell the property as provided in this chapter to the highest and best bidder for cash. (Sec. 84.64.080). The acceptable minimum bid shall be the total amount of taxes, interest, and costs.

Law: Revised Code of Washington, Title 84, Chapter 84.64, "Lien Foreclosure."

Contact: County Treasurer. The county treasurer shall be the receiver and collector of all taxes (Sec. 84.56.020).

Interest Rate: Not applicable. (Sec. 84.64.080)

Auction Type: Tax Deed (Sec. 84.64.080, Sec. 84.64.180).

Bidding Procedure: Premium bid / highest bid. (Sec. 84.64.080). Subject to the minimum bid requirement, the acceptable minimum bid shall be the total amount of taxes, interest, and costs, the property is sold to the highest and best bidder for cash (Sec. 84.64.080).

Costs: In addition to costs included in the minimum bid amount, the purchaser must pay a five-dollar fee for preparing and recording the deed (Sec. 84.64.215).

Redemption Period: Not applicable. (Sec. 84.64.060, Sec. 84.64.070).

Deed Assigned at Foreclosure to: The county treasurer shall execute to the purchaser of any piece or parcel of land a tax deed. (Sec. 84.64.080).

Wisconsin

Info for Wisconsin: This Tax Deed State sell their properties at Market value. This makes it extremely difficult to make a profit and eliminates discount of using tax lien and deed sales. This state will be extremely difficult to get a great deal on a property but anything is possible.

Summary: Annually, on September 1, the county treasurer shall issue to the county a tax certificate which includes all parcels of real property included in the tax roll for which real property taxes, special charges, special taxes or special assessments remain unpaid at the close of business on August 31. (Sec. 74.57) The County shall have the power to sell and convey its tax-deeded lands in such manner and upon such terms as the county board may by ordinance or resolution determine, including without restriction because of enumeration, sale by land contract, or by quitclaim or warranty deed with mortgage from vendee to secure any unpaid balance of the purchase price. (Sec. 75.35, Sec. 75.69).
Law: Wisconsin Statutes, Chapter 74, "Property Tax Collection," and Chapter 75, "Tax Sales."

Contact: County Treasurer. (Sec. 74.07). The taxation district treasurer and the county treasurer shall collect the general property taxes, special assessments, special taxes and special charges shown in the tax roll. (Sec.74.07).

Interest Rate: Not applicable.

Auction Type: Tax Deed. (Sec. 75.35, Sec. 75.69).

Bidding Procedure: Premium bid / highest bid. (Sec. 75.69). Any county may accept the bid most advantageous to it but every bid less than the appraised value of the property shall be rejected. Any county is authorized to sell for an amount equal to or above the appraised value, without re-advertising, any land previously advertised for sale. (Sec. 75.69).

Costs: Costs and fees payable by the purchaser at a tax sale are not specified by the Wisconsin state statutes.

Redemption Period: Not applicable.

Deed Assigned at Foreclosure to: The Purchaser at the tax sale (Sec. 75.35, Sec. 75.69).

 **BE FREE** UNIVERSITY   **Web Site:** https://befreeuniversity.com **Phone:** 855.5BE.FREE

Tax Liens

Tax Liens are a great investment if you are looking to get high returns on your investments, and aren't in a massive hurry to fuel the bank back up in a few months.

With Liens, there is always a waiting period called the redemption period. Each state has a different redemption period which we cover below. With Tax Liens You as the investor must wait till the owner of the property pays the liens, or the when the redemption period (determined by the state) expires. Then you can take action on that Lien.

We have found massive returns when you purchase a lien for pennies on the dollar that is work over $100,000 or more. If the homeowner does not redeem you can take possession of that property and flip or rent it.   This has happened more times than I can count however we must also acknowledge finding them for a little as $500 is rare but as noted very possible.

This has been our primary way of investing. Knowing what to look for that will determine the likelihood of redemption will greatly help your strategy whether you want the return of the interest rate or the property.

Side-note: Make sure to check with the county to see what is the process of obtaining deed to the parcel. You need to know and keep in mind if you have to foreclose on the property or does the county do it for you. Each county and state will be different however this is a must know so you know your time frames and cost of acquisition.

Tax Lien States

Alabama	Louisiana	Rhode Island
Arizona	Maryland	South Dakota
Colorado	Mississippi	Vermont
Illinois	Missouri	West Virgina
	Montana	Wyoming
Iowa	Nebraska	
Kentucky	New Jersey	

Alabama

Info for Alabama: This Tax Lien State has a long period of 3 years for redemption with a 12% Interest rate. Alabama does have an OTC "Over the Counter" sale that varies county-by-county.

Remember: When purchasing anything, you need to do you research and find out exactly what is going on with the property you are interested in: Location, Condition, Occupants, Assessed Value, Value of homes/property around it, etc. Do your due diligence, and you will reap the rewards.

Tax Sale Type: Tax Lien Certificates (Sec. 40-10-19   )

Contact: Tax Collector (Sec. 40-10-12 ⌐)

Interest Rate: 12% per annum (Sec. 40-10-122 ⌐)

BE FREE UNIVERSITY

Web Site: https://befreeuniversity.com **Phone:** 855.5BE.FREE

Penalty Rate: Not Applicable Not Applicable

Bid Procedure: Premium Bid (Sec. 40-10-16 ⬚)

Redemption Period: (3) three years (Sec. 40-10-29 ⬚)

Law: Code of Alabama, Title 40, Chapter 10, "Sale of Land."

Summary: After the court issues a decree (Sec. 40-10-11), properties with delinquent taxes are sold at an auction to the highest bidder for cash, between the hours of 10:00 A.M. and 4:00 P.M. (Sec. 40-10-15). The minimum bid is the amount decreed by the court, being delinquent taxes, interest, costs and penalties (Sec. 40-10-16).

 As soon after the confirmation of sale is made as may be practicable, the tax collector must make out and deliver to each purchaser, other than the state, a certificate of purchase (Sec. 40-10-19).
If no person shall bid for any real estate offered at such sale an amount sufficient to pay the sum specified in the decree of sale, and the costs and expenses subsequently accruing, the judge of probate shall bid in such real estate for the state at a price not exceeding the sum specified in such decree and such subsequently accruing
cost and expenses. (Sec. 40-10-18). A tax lien certificate is issued to the state, but the tax lien certificate may
subsequently be purchased directly from the State through assignment (Sec. 40-10-21).

Law: Code of Alabama, Title 40, Chapter 10, "Sale of Land."

Contact: County Tax

Collector: (Sec. 40-10-12).

Interest Rate: 12% per annum

(Sec. 40-10-122). "In order to obtain the redemption of land from tax sales where the same has been sold to one other than the state, the party desiring to make such redemption shall deposit with the judge of probate of the county in which the land is situated the amount of money for which the lands were sold, with interest thereon at

the rate of 12 percent per annum from date of sale." Both the minimum and premium bid amounts earn interest.

Auction Type: Tax Lien

Certificate (Sec. 40-10-19). "As soon after the confirmation of sale is made as may be practicable, the tax collector must make out and deliver to each purchaser, other than the state, a certificate of purchase, which shall contain a description of the real estate sold and show that the sum was assessed by the assessor, to whom assessed, the date of assessment, for what year or years the taxes were due, the amount of taxes thereon, the amount of and the name of the holder of each tax lien certificate related thereto, distinguishing the amount due the state and county and for school purposes and to each holder of a tax lien certificate and the fees and costs, that it was advertised and how long, that it was offered for sale and at what time, who became the purchaser, at what price and the fact and date of the confirmation of such sale."

Bidding Procedure: Premium bid / highest bid.

(Sec. 40-10-16).
Costs: The cost of advertising the part of such notices pertaining to lands purchased by others than the state shall be covered by the bids of the purchaser and collected by the collector as part of the purchase money (Sec. 40-10-23). When the purchaser returns the tax lien certificate a payment of a fee of $5 to the judge of probate will be required (Sec. 40-10-29).

Redemption Period: Three (3) years after the sale (Sec. 40-10-29). "After the expiration of three years from the date of the sale of any real estate for taxes, the judge of probate then in office must execute and deliver to the purchaser, other than the state, or person to whom the certificate of purchase has been assigned, upon the return of the certificate and payment of a fee of $5 to the judge of probate, a deed to each lot or parcel of real estate sold to the purchaser and remaining unredeemed."

Deed Assigned at Foreclosure to: Tax Lien Certificate holder (Sec. 40-10-29). "After the expiration of three (3) years from the date of the sale of any real estate for taxes, the judge of probate then in office must execute and deliver to the purchaser … a deed to each lot or parcel of real estate sold to the purchaser and remaining unredeemed … and such deed shall convey to and vest in the grantee all the right, title, interest and estate of the person whose duty it was to pay the taxes on such real estate and the lien and claim of the state and county thereto, but it shall not

Web Site: https://befreeuniversity.com **Phone:** 855.5BE.FREE

convey the right, title or interest of any reversioner or remainderman therein."
Notes: The deed conveyed upon expiration of the redemption period is not sufficient. You'll need to consult your legal professional for assistance with a quiet title action. Leftover liens not sold at the county level can be purchased from the Alabama State Commissioner of Revenue (Sec. 40-10-21 and 40-10-132)

Arizona

Info for Arizona: This Tax Lien State has a 3-year redemption period at an 16% Interest Rate. Tax Lien sales times vary by county but are usually held in May or June.

Summary: The tax lien sale shall be held in February of each year, each county auctions liens for properties that have delinquent taxes (Sec. 42-18112). A real property tax lien shall be sold pursuant to the person who pays the whole amount of delinquent taxes, interest, penalties and charges due on the property, and who in addition offers to accept the lowest rate of interest on the amount so paid to redeem the property from the sale, which may not exceed the rate prescribed by, and computed pursuant to, section 42-18053 (Sec. 42-18114).

If there is no bid for a tax lien, the county treasurer shall pass it for the time and shall reoffer it at the beginning of the sale on the next day until all tax liens are sold or until the county treasurer becomes satisfied that nou00a0more sales can be made. At that time the treasurer shall: 1. Assign to the state the property tax liens remaining unsold for the amount of the taxes, interest, penalties and charges. 2. Issue a certificate of purchase to the state as provided in other cases. (Sec. 42-18113), and if a tax lien is assigned to this state as provided by this article, the county treasurer shall sell, assign and deliver the certificate of purchase to any person who pays to the county treasurer the whole amount then due under the certificate, including interest, penalties and charges, and in addition the entire amount of subsequent taxes assessed on the property described in the certificate (Sec. 42-18122).

Law: Arizona Revised Statutes Annotated, Title 42, Chapter 18, u201cCollection and Enforcement.u201d
Contact: County Treasurer (Sec. 42-18101). u201cThe county treasurer shall secure

Web Site: https://befreeuniversity.com **Phone:** 855.5BE.FREE

the payment of unpaid delinquent taxes by using the provisions of this article and articles 4, 5 and 6 of this chapter to sell the tax liens provided for in section 42-17154 and to foreclose the right to redeem. u201d

Interest Rate: 16% per annum (Sec. 42-18053). u201c Except as provided in subsection B, all taxes bear interest from the time of delinquency at the rate of sixteen per cent per year simple until paid. A fraction of a month is counted as a whole month. B. Interest shall not be collected: 1. If the delinquency is the result of an error by the county assessor or county treasurer. 2. If the full year tax for the year is paid on or before December 31 of the tax year. u201d

Auction Type: Tax Lien Certificate (Sec. 42-18118). u201c The county treasurer shall make, execute and deliver a certificate of purchase to each purchaser at the sale for delinquent taxes or to each assignee…u201d

Bidding Procedure: Bid down the interest rate

(Sec. 42-188114). u201cA real property tax lien shall be sold pursuant to this article to the person who pays the whole amount of delinquent taxes, interest, penalties and charges due on the property, and who in addition offers to accept the lowest rate of interest on the amount so paid to redeem the property from the sale, which may not exceed the rate prescribed by, and computed pursuant to, section 42-18053.u201d

Costs: The county treasurer shall collect from the purchaser or assignee a fee of $10 for each certificate (Sec.42-18118), the county treasurer shall collect a fee of five dollars from the holder of the certificate for makingu00a0the entries when payment for delinquent taxes are made. (Sec. 42-18121), a $10 fee per parcel for delivery ofu00a0deed (Sec. 42-18205). At the time of applying for a treasureru2019s deed, the purchaser or the purchaseru2019s assigns shall pay to the county treasurer a fee of five dollars and the estimated costs of the title search, of publishingu00a0notice, of mailing notice and of posting notice on the property as provided by this article. (Sec. 42-18252).

Redemption Period: Within three (3) years after the date of the sale (Sec. 42-18152). u201cAt any time beginning three years after the sale of a tax lien but not later than ten years after the last day of the month in which the lien was acquired, if the lien is not redeemed, the purchaser or the purchaseru2019s heirs or assigns, or the state
if it is the assignee, may bring an action in superior court in the county in which the real property is located to foreclose the right to redeem (42-18201). A real property

tax lien may be redeemed at any time after three years but before the delivery of a treasureru2019s deed to the purchaser or the purchaseru2019s heirs or assigns. u201d

Deed Assigned at Foreclosure to: Tax Certificate holder (Sec. 42-18204). u201c In an action to foreclose the right to redeem, if the court finds that the sale is valid, and that the tax lien has not been redeemed, the court shall enter judgment:
1. Foreclosing the right of the defendant to redeem.
2. Directing the county treasurer to expeditiously execute and deliver to the party in whose favor judgment is entered, including the state, a deed conveying the property described in the certificate of purchase.
B. After entering judgment the parties whose rights to redeem the tax lien are thereby foreclosed have no further legal or equitable right, title or interest in the property subject to the right of appeal and stay of execution as in other civil actions.
C. The foreclosure of the right to redeem does not extinguish any easement on or appurtenant to the property. D. The foreclosure of the right to redeem does not extinguish any lien for an assessment levied pursuant to title
48, chapter 4, 6 or 14, or section 9-276.u201d
NOTE: Real estate tax liens do NOT take priority over state liens.

Colorado

Info for Colorado: This Tax Lien State redemption period is 3 years with a 9% interest rate. Colorado is a state where you must know how to analyze properties and know how to do in depth research. We cover all of these in our Tax Lien Master Class.

Colorado has in person bidding and also online bidding. If you are interested in bidding in Colorado's online auctions visit www.realauction.com and www.sri-auctionsonline.com.

Summary: The sale of tax liens on lands upon which taxes remain delinquent shall commence on or before the second Monday in December of each year and shall be held at the treasurer's office in each county or at any other location in the county deemed suitable by the treasurer; (Sec. 39-11-109). Setting a minimum total of taxes, delinquent interest, and costs below which competitive bids will not be accepted. (Sec. 39-11-115). Interest is paid only on the minimum bid and on subsequent taxes paid by the purchaser. It is important to note that you will not

collect interest on any amounts in excess of the delinquent taxes (Sec. 39-12-103). Any Bid in excess will be credited to the county general fund.

If there is no bid for any tax lien offered, the offering of such tax lien shall remain open until all the tax liens are offered for sale and the sale is ended or until the treasurer is satisfied that no more sales can be affected, whereupon it is his duty to strike off to the county, city, town, or city and county the tax liens on those lands and town lots remaining unsold, for the amount of such taxes, delinquent interest, and costs thereon. (Sec. 39-11-108).

Law: Colorado Revised Statutes, Title 39, Article 11 (Sales of Tax Liens) and Article 12 (Redemption).
Contact: The County Treasurer (Sec. 39-11-101).
Interest Rate: +9% per annum (Sec. 39-12-103 (3)).
"The annual rate of redemption interest shall be nine percentage points above the discount rate, which discount rate shall be the rate of interest a commercial bank pays to the federal reserve bank of Kansas City using a government bond or other eligible paper as security, and shall be rounded to the nearest full percent. On September 1 of each year, the annual rate of redemption interest shall be established in the same manner, to become effective on October 1 of the same year."

Auction Type: Tax Lien Certificate (Sec. 39-11-117). Furthermore (Sec. 39-11-109), "The sale of tax liens on lands upon which taxes remain delinquent shall commence on or before the second Monday in December of each year and shall be held at the treasurer's office in each county or at any other location in the county deemed suitable by the treasurer; except that all of the property offered for sale on the same day shall be offered for sale at the same location."

Bidding Procedure: Premium bid / highest bid. (Sec. 39-11-115). "When the taxes levied for the preceding year or years on any lands remain unpaid, the tax liens on such lands offered at public auction at the times provided by law shall be sold to the persons who pay therefor the taxes, delinquent interest, and fees then due thereon or who further pay the largest amount in excess of said taxes, delinquent interest, and fees. The excess amount shall be credited to the county general fund." However, according to (Sec. 39-11-115 (2)), "In order that the public auction may be conducted in an efficient and equitable manner, the treasurer is hereby granted broad powers to set bidding rules governing the public auction. Such powers shall include, but need not be limited to, the following:
(a) Recognition of buyers in numerical sequence, in rotation, or in the order in which bids are made;

(b) Determining the order in which tax liens are sold, without regard to the order in which they appear in the published notice of sale;

(c) Setting minimum bid increases; and

(d) Setting a minimum total of taxes, delinquent interest, and costs below which competitive bids will not be accepted.

(3) The treasurer may combine and sell as a unit parcel which are contiguous or are contained within one subdivision.

(4) The treasurer shall announce bidding rules at the beginning of the public auction, and the rules announced shall apply to all bidders throughout the public auction. If the public auction is conducted by means of the internet or other electronic medium, the treasurer shall cause the internet bidding rules to be posted on the medium for at least two weeks before the date of sale. The internet bidding rules posted shall apply to all bidders throughout the public auction."

Costs: For each certificate of purchase delivered, four dollars (Sec. 39-11-117), $5 for payment of subsequent taxes (Sec. 39-11-119), and $75 fee for deed application ($35 if not advertised) (Sec. 39-11-120).

Redemption Period: Three (3) years (Sec. 39-11-120). Real property for which a tax lien was sold under the provisions of article 11 of this title as a result of delinquent taxes may be redeemed by the owner thereof or his agent, assignee, or attorney, or by any person having a legal or equitable claim therein, or by a holder of a tax sale certificate; except that such holder may redeem such real property from any sale of a tax lien thereof made subsequent to the time of the issuance of the tax sale certificate upon which he is relying, and the amount paid for the redemption of the subsequent certificate of purchase shall be endorsed as subsequent taxes paid on the certificate upon which he is relying.(Sec. 39-12-103). The purchaser may apply for a deed once three years have passed from the date of the sale.

Deed Assigned at Foreclosure to: Tax Lien Certificate holder (Sec. 39-11-120). "At any time after the expiration of the term of three years from the date of the sale of any tax lien on any land, or interest therein or improvements thereon, for delinquent taxes, on demand of the purchaser or lawful holder of the certificate of such tax lien, other than the county wherein such property is situated, and on presentation of such certificate of purchase or properly authenticated order of the board of county commissioners, where the certificate has been lost or wrongfully withheld from the owner, and upon proof of compliance with section 39-11-128 the treasurer shall make out a deed for each such lot, parcel, interest, or improvement

for which a tax lien was sold and which remains unredeemed and deliver the same to such purchaser or lawful holder of such certificate or order."

Notes: According to (Sec. 39-11-115 New Window) the overbid does not draw interest. Furthermore, the overbid will not be returned upon redemption and "shall be credited to the county general fund".

Illinois

Info for Illinois: In this Tax Lien State the redemption period is 2 years and the interest varies depending on the type of land; the investor will receive 24% on farm land and 36% on any other land amortized over a entire year.

Summary: Not less than 15 days before the date of application for judgment and sale of delinquent properties, the county collector shall mail, by registered or certified mail, a notice of the forthcoming application for judgment and sale (Sec. 21-110, Sec. 21-135), The collector, in person or by deputy, shall attend, on the day and in the place specified in the notice for the sale of property for taxes, and shall, between 9:00 a.m. and 4:00 p.m., or later at the collector's discretion, proceed to offer for sale, separately and in consecutive order, all property in the list on which the taxes, special assessments, interest or costs have not been paid (Sec. 21-205). Every property offered at public sale, and not sold for want of bidders, unless it is released from sale by the withdrawal from collection of a special assessment levied thereon, shall be forfeited to the State of Illinois (Sec. 21-225). If taxes on a property have been delinquent for two years or longer, the county may apply to have the tax lien certificates sold at a scavenger sale all properties shall be offered for sale in consecutive order as they appear in the delinquent list. The minimum bid for any property shall be $250 or one-half of the tax if the total liability is less than $500 (Sec. 21-260).

Law: Illinois Compiled Statutes, Chapter 35, Title 7, "Tax Collection" (35 ILCS 200/21-5 et seq.).
Contact: The county tax collector (Sec. 21-110).
Interest Rate: 18% penalty (Sec. 21-215).
Auction Type: Tax Lien Certificate (Sec. 21-240).
Bidding Procedure: Bid down the penalty (Regular tax sales) (Sec. 21-215) and the highest/greatest bid (for Scavenger tax sales) (Sec. 21-260).

Costs: $10 automation fee (Sec. 21-245).

Redemption Period: Two (2) to three (3) years (Sec. 21-350). "Property sold under this Code may be redeemed at any time before the expiration of 2 years from the date of sale, except that:

(a) If on the date of sale, the property is vacant non-farm property or property containing an improvement consisting of a structure or structures with 7 or more residential units or that is commercial or industrial property, it may be redeemed at any time before the expiration of 6 months from the date of sale if the property, at the time of sale, was for each of 2 or more years delinquent or forfeited for all or part of the general taxes due on the property.

(b) If on the date of sale, the property sold was improved with a structure consisting of at least one and not more than 6 dwelling units it may be redeemed at any time on or before the expiration of 2 years and 6 months from the date of sale. If, however, the court that ordered the property sold, upon the verified petition of the holder of the certificate of purchase brought within 4 months from the date of sale, finds and declares that the structure on the property is abandoned, then the court may order that the property may be redeemed at any time on or before the expiration of 2 years from the date of sale. Notice of the hearing on a petition to declare the property abandoned shall be given to the owner or owners of the property and to the person in whose name the taxes were last assessed, by certified or registered mail sent to their last known addresses at least 5 days before the date of the hearing.

(c) If the period of redemption has been extended by the certificate holder as provided in Section 21-385, the property may be redeemed on or before the extended redemption date."

Deed Assigned at Foreclosure to: The Tax Lien Certificate holder (Sec. 21-205). "The collector, in person or by deputy, shall attend, on the day and in the place specified in the notice for the sale of property for taxes, and shall, between 9:00 a.m. and 4:00 p.m., or later at the collector's discretion, proceed to offer for sale, separately and in consecutive order, all property in the list on which the taxes, special assessments, interest or costs have not been paid. However, in any county with 3,000,000 or more inhabitants, the offer for sale shall be made between 8:00 a.m. and 8:00 p.m. The collector's office shall be kept open during all hours in which the sale is in progress. The sale shall be continued from day to day, until all property in the delinquent list has been offered for sale. However, any city, village or incorporated town interested in the collection of any tax or special assessment, may, in default of bidders, withdraw from collection the special assessment levied against any property by the corporate authorities of the city, village or incorporated

town. In case of a withdrawal, there shall be no sale of that property on account of the delinquent special assessment thereon.

In every sale of property pursuant to the provisions of this Code, the collector may employ any automated means that the collector deems appropriate, provided that bidders are required to personally attend the sale. The changes made by this amendatory Act of the 94th General Assembly are declarative of existing law."

Notes:

Penalty rate: The person at the sale offering to pay the amount due on each property for the least percentage shall be the purchaser of that property. No bid shall be accepted for a penalty exceeding the maximum of 18% (Sec. 21-215). For Regular Tax Sales, the penalty percentage is then computed through the date of redemption as a percentage of the certificate amount, as follows (Sec. 21-355):

Redeemed within 06 months – penalty bid at sale;
Redeemed within 12 months – two times the penalty interest rate bid;
Redeemed within 18 months – three times the penalty interest rate bid;
Redeemed within 24 months – four times the penalty interest rate bid;
Redeemed within 36 months – five times the penalty interest rate bid.

The person redeeming from Scavenger tax sales shall pay interest on that part of the amount for which the property was sold equal to or less than the full amount of delinquent taxes, special assessments, penalties, interest, and costs, included in the judgment and order of sale as follows:

(1) If redeemed within the first 2 months from the date of the sale, 3% per month upon the amount of taxes, special assessments, penalties, interest, and costs due for each of the first 2 months or fraction thereof. (2) If redeemed at any time between 2 and 6 months from the date of the sale, 12% of the amount of taxes, special assessments, penalties, interest, and costs due. (3) If redeemed at any time between 6 and 12 months from the date of the sale, 24% of the amount of taxes, special assessments, penalties, interest, and costs due. (4) If redeemed at any time between 12 and 18 months from the date of the sale, 36% of the amount of taxes, special assessments, penalties, interest, and costs due. (5) If redeemed at any time between 18 and 24 months from the date of the sale, 48% of the amount of taxes, special assessments, penalties, interest, and costs due. (6) If redeemed after 24 months from the date of sale, the 48% provided for the 24 months together with interest at 6% per annum thereafter on the amount of taxes, special assessments, penalties, interest and costs due (Sec.21-260).

 **BE FREE** UNIVERSITY

Web Site: https://befreeuniversity.com **Phone:** 855.5BE.FREE

Important. According to (Sec. 21-260) 'The person redeeming shall not be required to pay any interest on any part of the amount for which the property was sold that exceeds the full amount of delinquent taxes, special assessments, penalties, interest, and costs included in the judgment and order of sale.' Basically, this means that anything over and above the minimum bid will not draw interest.

Redemption period: Generally, properties may be redeemed at any time before the expiration of 2 years from the date of sale, (Sec. 21-350). However, the owner of a tax lien certificate can extend the redemption to three years from the date of sale (Sec. 21-385).

Attaining a Tax Deed: At any time within 5 months but not less than 3 months prior to the expiration of the redemption period for property sold pursuant to judgment and order of sale under Sections 21-110 through 21-120 or 21-260, the purchaser or his or her assignee may file a petition in the circuit court in the same proceeding in which the judgment and order of sale were entered, asking that the court direct county clerk to issue a tax deed if the property is not redeemed from the sale. The petition shall be accompanied by the statutory filing fee.

Notice of filing the petition and the date on which the petitioner intends to apply for an order on the petition that a deed be issued if the property is not redeemed shall be given to occupants, owners and persons interested in the property as part of the notice provided in Sections 22-10 through 22-25, except that only one publication is required. The county clerk shall be notified of the filing of the petition and any person owning or interested in the property may, if he or she desires, appear in the proceeding.

You MUST record your Tax Deed: Unless the holder of the certificate purchased at any tax sale under this Code takes out the deed in the time provided by law, and records the same within one year from and after the time for redemption expires, the certificate or deed, and the sale on which it is based, shall, after the expiration of the one-year period, be absolutely void with no right to reimbursement. If the holder of the certificate is prevented from obtaining a deed by injunction or order of any court, or by the refusal or inability of any court to act upon the application for a tax deed, or by the refusal of the clerk to execute the same deed, the time he or she is so prevented shall be excluded from computation of the one-year period. Certificates of purchase and deeds executed by the clerk shall recite the qualifications required in this Section (Sec. 22-85).

Web Site: https://befreeuniversity.com **Phone:** 855.5BE.FREE

Iowa

Info for Iowa: This Tax Lien State has a 2-year redemption period with a maximum 24% interest. This state is different as it requires the investor to bid down what percentage of the property you own.

If the property redeems, this is fantastic, but if it doesn't, there is a situation where you own part of the property and the homeowner does as well. Not all counties are like this, so be sure to check and find ones that aren't and really cash in on those great interest rates. (And shorter redemption period.)

Summary: Annually, on the third Monday in June the county treasurer shall offer at public sale all parcels on which taxes are delinquent. The sale shall be made for the total amount of taxes, interest, fees, and costs due. If for good cause the treasurer cannot hold the annual tax sale on the third Monday of June, the treasurer may designate a different date in June for the sale. (Sec. 446.7, Sec. 446.15). The minimum bid is the amount
of delinquent property taxes, interest, penalties and costs (Sec. 446.7). When a parcel is offered at a tax sale under section 446.18, and no bid is received, or if the bid received is less than the total amount due, the county in which the parcel is located, through its county treasurer, shall bid for the parcel a sum equal to the total amount due (Sec. 446.19).
Law: Code of Iowa, Title X, Subtitle 2, Chapter 446, "Tax Sales," Chapter 447, "Tax Redemption," and Chapter
448, "Tax Deeds."

Contact: The County Treasurer (Sec. 446.7).
Interest Rate: 2% per month (24% per annum). More specifically, A parcel sold under this chapter and chapter 446 may be redeemed at any time before the right of redemption expires, by payment to the county treasurer, to be held by the treasurer subject to the order of the purchaser, of the amount for which the parcel was sold, including the fee for the certificate of purchase, and interest of two percent per month, counting each
fraction of a month as an entire month, from the month of sale, and the total amount paid by the purchaser or the purchaser's assignee for any subsequent year, with interest at the same rate added on the amount of the payment for each subsequent year from the month of payment, counting each fraction of a month as an entire month (Sec. 447.1).

Web Site: https://befreeuniversity.com **Phone:** 855.5BE.FREE

Auction Type: Tax Lien Certificate (Sec. 446.1). "The county treasurer shall designate on the county system each parcel sold for taxes and not redeemed, by noting on the county system the year in which it was sold."

Bidding Procedure: Premium bid / highest bid. (Sec. 446.16). "The person who offers to pay the total amount due, which is a lien on any parcel, for the smallest percentage of the parcel is the purchaser, and when the purchaser designates the percentage of any parcel for which the purchaser will pay the total amount due, the percentage thus designated shall give the person an undivided interest upon the issuance of a treasurer's deed/"

Costs: Statutory costs collectible as part of the sale price include up to $4 for publishing the notice of sale (Sec.446.10) and a "reasonable" registration fee (Sec. 446.16).

Redemption Period: Two (2) years (see notes). A parcel sold under this chapter and chapter 446 may be redeemed at any time before the right of redemption expires, by payment to the county treasurer, (Sec. 447.1). After one year and nine months from the date of sale, or after nine months from the date of a sale made under section 446.18, 446.19A, or 446.39, the holder of the certificate of purchase may cause to be served upon the person in possession of the parcel, and also upon the person in whose name the parcel is taxed, a notice signed by the certificate holder or the certificate holder's agent or attorney, stating the date of sale, the description of the parcel sold, the name of the purchaser, and that the right of redemption will expire and a deed for the parcel be made unless redemption is made within ninety days from the completed service of the notice (Sec. 447.9).

Deed Assigned at Foreclosure to: Tax Lien Certificate holder (Sec. 448.1). Immediately after the expiration of ninety days from the date of completed service of the notice provided in section 447.12, the county treasurer shall make out a deed for each parcel sold and unredeemed upon the return of the certificate of purchase and payment of the appropriate deed and recording fees by the purchaser.

Notes: Important: According to Iowa statute, after one year and nine months from the date of the sale, the holder of the tax lien certificate is required to serve a notice stating that the right of redemption will expire and a deed for the parcel be made unless redemption is made within ninety days from the completed service of the notice (Sec. 447.9).

Web Site: https://befreeuniversity.com **Phone:** 855.5BE.FREE

After three years from the date of the sale, if the county determines that the holder of the tax lien certificate has failed to serve the 90-day notice the tax lien certificate will be void. Furthermore, the money paid to purchase the tax lien certificate will be credited to the county's general fund (Sec. 448.12).

Kentucky

Info for Kentucky: This Tax Lien State has a 1-year redemption period and a 12% redemption rate. You will find that most counties in Kentucky have different bidding processes, some are unique only to Kentucky. All bidding process are covered in our Tax Lien Master Class.

The investor in Kentucky must go through a foreclosure process. While going through this process a judge could determine that property must go to a foreclosure sale, which would mean you would receive the money you invested on the lien. This doesn't sound fair but I didn't write the rules for this state.

Summary: After the sheriff has exhausted all the delinquent taxpayer's personal property, tax claims on real property may be sold to collect delinquent property taxes (Sec. 134.430). Tax claim sales are held during April. Any property while owned by the tax delinquent home owner shall be subject to distrait or an action in persona, or both, to enforce the obligation, and shall also be subject to distrait or levy as provided in

subsection (1) of KRS 134.430, but no action may be brought to enforce a certificate of delinquency until one (1) year after the issuance thereof, and the action shall be instituted with (10) years after the expiration of that one (1) year period (Sec. 134.470, Sec. 134.490).

Law: Kentucky Revised Statutes, Title IX, Chapter 91, Section 91.420 et seq., "Collection – Tax Sale" (Louisville); Title XI, Chapter 134, "Payment, Collection, and Refund of Taxes."

Contact: Local Tax Collector (usually the sheriff) (Sec. 134.450).
Interest Rate: 12% per annum (Sec. 134.490). "Within fifty (50) days after the issuance of a certificate of delinquency to a private purchaser, the private purchaser

shall give the same notice as required of a county attorney in KRS 134.500(2)." According to (Sec. 134.500(3)(a)), "The notice shall advise the owner, and bears interest at the rate of twelve percent (12%) per annum, and if the certificate is not paid, it will be subject to collection as provided by law."

Auction Type: Tax Lien Certificate/Tax claims (Sec. 134.430). Furthermore, all personal property owned by a delinquent taxpayer shall be subject to distrait, and all property owned by him shall be subject to levy and sale by the proper collecting officer at any time from February 1 after the claim becomes delinquent until the tax claim is barred by limitations, unless otherwise provided by law.

Bidding Procedures: Premium bid / highest bid. (Sec. 134.450). "Tax claims are sold to the purchaser who first offers to pay the full amount of the delinquent property taxes and fees."

Costs: As compensation for his/her services, the sheriff shall be entitled to an additional ten percent (10%) of that part of the tax claim represented by the total taxes plus ten percent (10%) penalty, for all delinquent taxes collected from the time the (10%) penalty becomes applicable through the sale of the tax claims. This fee shall be added to the total amount due and paid by the person paying the delinquent tax bill (Sec. 134.430). As compensation for his/her services, the sheriff shall receive five dollars ($5) for each tax claim advertised. (Sec.134.440).

Redemption Period: One (1) year (Sec. 134.470). "An uncollectible tax bill or a certificate of delinquency shall embrace the entire tax claim, including the lien provided in subsection (1) of KRS 134.420, and shall continue to be a personal obligation of the delinquent taxpayer. Any property while owned by him shall be subject to foreclosure or execution in satisfaction of a judgment pursuant to an action in rem or an action in persona, or both, to enforce the obligation, and shall also be subject to distrait or levy as provided in subsection (1) of KRS 134.430, but no action may be brought to enforce a certificate of delinquency until one (1) year after the issuance thereof, and the action shall be instituted within ten (10) years after the expiration of that one (1) year period. During the one (1) year period the statute of limitations shall be suspended in all respects and shall be continued in all respects for ten (10) years thereafter. If the owner of a certificate of delinquency proceeds to enforce satisfaction of the certificate, he may include all other certificates held by him against the same delinquent taxpayer; but insofar as the proceedings may undertake to affect a lien foreclosure, they shall be governed

Web Site: https://befreeuniversity.com **Phone:** 855.5BE.FREE

by the time applicable to the particular property subject to the lien, if that property is no longer owned by the delinquent."

Deed Assigned at Foreclosure to: The tax sale purchaser (Sec. 134.490).
Notes: According to (Sec. 134.490), "the purchaser must, within 50 days after the purchase of a certificate of delinquency (tax lien certificate) give 'notice' according to the stipulations outlined in Sec. 134.490 New Window to the owner of the tax delinquent property."

Louisiana

Info for Louisiana: This Tax Lien State is a 3-year redemption period with interest rates starting a 100% but then bid down to the lowest percentage down to 1%.

Louisiana has adjudicated properties that act like OTC properties. You may find it beneficial to look into these properties.

Some counties have gone to online sales which can be found at www.civicsource.com.

Summary: The tax collectors throughout the state of Louisiana shall seize, advertise and sell the property upon which delinquent taxes are due, on or before the first day of May of the year following the year in which the taxes were assessed, or as soon thereafter as possible (Sec. 47:2182). The minimum bid is delinquent taxes, interest, penalties, and costs (Sec. 47:2184). The winning bidder receives a deed to the property, subject to the three years right of redemption (Sec. 47:2183a). If there is no minimum bid, the tax collector shall bid in the property for the state (Sec. 47:2186, La R.S., par. 96-334); however, if property located in a municipality with a population of more than four hundred fifty thousand persons as of the most recent federal decennial census fails to sell for the minimum required bid in the tax sale, the collector may offer the property for sale at a subsequent sale with no minimum required bid. The proceeds of the sale shall be applied to the taxes, interest, and costs due on the property, and any remaining deficiency shall be eliminated from the tax rolls. (Const.Sec. 25).

Law: Louisiana Constitution, Article VII, Sec. 25, "Tax Sales." Louisiana Revised Statutes, Title 47, Subtitle III, Chapter 5, "Tax Sales and Redemptions."

Contact: Parish or municipal tax collector (Sec. 47:2182). "The tax collectors throughout the state shall seize, advertise and sell the property upon which delinquent taxes are due."

Interest Rate: One (1%) per month (12% per annum) plus a 5% penalty (Sec. 47:2222). "The person redeeming property, in whole or in part, shall pay all taxes assessed upon the property redeemed subsequent to the tax sale with interest at the rate of one percent per month until redeemed. The property sold shall be redeemable for three years after the date of recordation of the tax sale, by paying the price given, including costs, five percent penalty thereon, and interest at the rate of one percent per month until redemption."

Auction Type: Hybrid Tax Deed (Sec. 47:2183).

Bidding Procedure: Premium bid / highest bid. (Sec. 47:2184). "If the property is divisible and a portion of the property is sufficient to satisfy the amounts owed, the collector must require bids to be for such lesser portion of the property."

Costs: Statutory costs included in the minimum bid requirements include the cost of providing notices of delinquency (Sec. 47:2171, Sec. 47:2180). Other costs and fees are not specified by Louisiana Statute.

Redemption Period: Three (3) years. (Sec. 47:2183 (a)) "A. Each state tax collector and ex officio collector of state taxes, and the tax collectors of the municipal authorities of the various towns and city governments and political subdivisions throughout the state, shall execute and sign in person or by deputy, in the name of the state, or other taxing subdivision as the case may be, a deed of sale to purchasers of any real estate sold for taxes, in which he shall relate in substance a brief history of the proceedings had, shall describe the property, state the amount of the taxes, interest, and costs and the bid made for the property, and the payment made to him in cash, cashier's check, certified check, money order, or wire transfer, and shall sell the property to the purchaser, with the right to be placed in actual possession thereof, by order of a court of competent jurisdiction, and shall conclude the deed with the statement that the property shall be redeemable at any time for the space of three years beginning on the day when the deed is filed for record in the conveyance office in the parish in which the property is situated."

Deed Assigned at Foreclosure to: Tax sale purchaser. (Sec. 47:2183) "If not redeemed, such record in the conveyance or mortgage office shall operate as a

Web Site: https://befreeuniversity.com **Phone**: 855.5BE.FREE

cancellation of all conventional and judicial mortgages; provided that whenever a sale shall be made at the instance and request of a subrogate as provided in R.S. 47:2105, the recordation in the conveyance or mortgage office of the tax deed executed by the tax collector to the purchaser shall operate as a cancellation of all liens and privileges, as well as of all conventional and judicial mortgages, recorded against the property sold, except the liens and privileges for taxes and paving and other assessments due the state or any political subdivision thereof which shall be governed by existing laws."

Notes: Record the Tax Deed. According to (Sec. 47:2183 (A)) the purchaser must file the deed 'for record in the conveyance office in the parish in which the property is situated.' to begin the countdown of home owners three (3) year right to redeem. Obtaining a writ of possession. Louisiana is unique in that the purchaser of the hybrid tax deed can request immediate possession of the property before the expiration of the home owners three (3) year right to redeem has expired. Sec. 47:2185 Immovable property; putting in possession 'Upon the presentation of a certified copy of a tax deed for immovables to any judge of competent jurisdiction (such jurisdiction to be determined by the value of the immovables therein described and not the amount of the taxes), the judge shall in chambers grant an order of seizure and possession, commanding the sheriff to seize such property and place the purchaser in actual possession thereof; a writ of possession shall be issued thereon by the clerk, but the purchaser may take actual possession without such order, with the consent or acquiescence of the tax debtor or otherwise, provided no force or violence shall be used.'

Maryland

Info for Maryland: This state has a redemption of 6 months up to 2 years with interest rates that range between 6% to 24% and varies on each county.

There are a few major counties in Maryland that you should look into investing in: Baltimore City, Frederick County, Harford County, Howard County and Montgomery County are a few to start in.

Summary: Following notice. At any time after 30 days from the mailing of the statement and notice, the collector shall cause to be published, 4 times, once a week

for 4 successive weeks in 1 or more newspapers that have a general circulation in the county in which the property is located, a notice that the property will, on the date and at the place named in the notice, be sold at public auction (Sec. 14-813). All sales shall be at public auction to the person who makes the highest good faith accepted bid, in fee or leasehold, as the case may be. (Sec. 14-808, Sec. 14-817). The minimum bid is the amount of past due taxes, interest, penalties and costs. If there is no bid for the property then, the governing body of a county or other taxing agency shall buy in and hold any property in their respective counties offered for sale for nonpayment of any taxes for which there is no private purchaser. (Sec. 14-824). The purchaser receives a certificate of purchase (Sec. 14-817), and may petition for foreclosure after six (6) months (Sec. 14-833).

Law: Annotated Code of Maryland, Tax-Property Article, Title 14, Subtitle 8, Part III, "Tax Sales."
Contact: Local tax collector (Sec. 14-808).
Interest Rate: Generally, 6% to 24% (Baltimore City). Varies by city (Sec. 14-820, Sec. 14-828).
Auction Type: Tax Lien Certificate (Sec. 14-820).
Bidding Procedure: Premium bid / highest bid. (Sec. 14-817). "A bidder raises the amount above the minimum amount due."
Costs: Statutory costs vary from county to county and may be found in statute http://mlis.state.md.us/cgi-win/
web_statutes.exe (Sec. 14-813).

Redemption Period: Six (6) months (Sec. 14-833). "The owner of the Tax Lien Certificate at any time after 6 months from the date of sale a holder of any certificate of sale may file a complaint to foreclose all rights of redemption of the property to which the certificate relates. The certificate is void unless a proceeding to foreclose the right of redemption is filed within 2 years of the date of the certificate of sale."

Deed Assigned at Foreclosure to: Tax lien certificate holder (Sec. 14-847). "The judgment of the court shall direct the collector to execute a deed to the holder of the certificate of sale in fee simple or in leasehold, as appropriate, on payment to the collector of the balance of the purchase price, due on account of the purchase price of the property, together with all taxes and interest and penalties on the property that accrue after the date of sale. The judgment shall direct the supervisor to enroll the holder of the certificate of sale in fee simple or in leasehold, as appropriate, as the owner of the property."

Notes: According to (Sec. 14-830) the 'owner of any property sold under the provisions of this subtitle shall have the right, during the period of redemption, to continue in possession of, and to exercise all rights of ownership over the property until the right of redemption has been finally foreclosed...'

Attaining a Tax Deed: According to (Sec. 14-833) the owner of a tax lien certificate can file for a tax deed six (6) months after the purchase of the tax lien but no later than two (2) years from the date the tax lien certificate was purchased.

Mississippi

Info for Mississippi: This Tax Lien State has a redemption period of 2 years with a 18% per year interest rate. In this state Sales Tax Sales usually held in August on the last Monday.

Statute Summary: Except as otherwise provided in Sec. 27-41-2, after the fifth day of August in each year hereafter, the tax collector shall advertise all lands in his county on which all the taxes due and in arrears have not been paid, as provided by law, as well as all land which is liable to sale for the other taxes which have matured, as required by law, for sale at the door of the courthouse of his county or any place within the courthouse that the tax collector deems suitable to hold such sale, provided that the place of such sale shall be designated by the tax collector in the advertisement of the notice of tax sale on the last Monday of August. (Sec. 27-41-55). The sale of real estate for ad valorem taxes and special improvement assessments and sale of personal property shall be made upon the same notice, at the same time, and in the same manner as provided by law for sales of like property for unpaid state and county taxes. (Sec. 21-33-63).

Upon the written request of any taxpayer owing taxes on any property to any fund whatsoever, collection whereof is to be made by such tax collector, to assign in writing to any assignee named by such taxpayer, all lien or liens for taxes thus to be collected, in favor of the state, county or municipality, improvement or school or levee district, or other taxing district, upon the payment to such tax collector of such taxes then owing, due and unpaid, together with all costs or damages that may have been incurred thereon, and to attach the official receipt to such assignments. (Sec. 27-47-1). It shall be lawful for any person paying the taxes for another, at his request, and procuring an assignment of such lien as herein provided, to make an interest charge of not more than ten per cent per annum upon the amount of taxes,

costs and damages which have accrued against the property or person causing the assignment to be made, and the assignee shall have for said charge the same lien as the lien for taxes. (Sec. 27-47-7) At any time after the expiration of six months from the date of such assignment, the assignee of said lien may in writing direct the tax collector who made the assignment or his successor in office, to enforce the said lien. (Sec. 27-47-13) In addition to the remedies hereinbefore provided, the owner of said certificate of assignment shall have the right to enforce such collection of same in any court of competent jurisdiction by instituting action to enforce the lien on the property against which said taxes have been assessed, and by personal judgment against the person who requested payment of said taxes. (Sec. 27-47-21).

Law: Mississippi Code, Title 21, Chapter 33, Article 1, "Taxation" (municipal) and Title 27, Chapter 41, "Ad Valorem Taxes — Collection", Chapter 45, "Ad Valorem Taxes — Redemption of Land Sold for Taxes," and Chapter 47, "Ad Valorem Taxes — Assignment of Tax Liens."
Contact: Local Tax Collectors (Sec. 27-41-47).

Interest Rate: 18% per annum and 5% penalty (Sec. 27-45-3). The specific interest return varies upon when it is actually redeemed. The cost to redeem property includes the amount of all taxes for which the land was sold, with all costs incident to the sale, and five percent (5%) damages on the amount of taxes for which the land was sold, and interest on all such taxes and costs at the rate of one and one-half percent (1-1/2%) per month, or any fractional part thereof, from the date of such sale, and all costs that have accrued on the land since the sale, with interest thereon from the date such costs shall have accrued, at the rate of one and one-half percent (1-1/2%) per month, or any fractional part thereof; (Sec. 27-45-3).
If the land be redeemed, or the title of the purchaser be defeated or set aside in any way or for any reason, such excess shall be retained by the county. If the owner of the property does not request payment of the excess within two (2) years from the expiration of the period of redemption, the excess shall be retained by the county (Sec. 27-41-77).

Auction Type: Tax Lien Certificate (Sec. 27-41-55). When the period of redemption has expired, the chancery clerk shall, on demand, execute deeds of conveyance to individuals purchasing lands at tax sales. (Sec. 27-45-23).

Bidding Procedure: Premium bid / highest bid. (Sec. 27-41-59). The tax collector shall proceed to sell, for the payment of taxes then remaining due and unpaid, together with all fees, penalties and damages provided by law, the land or so much

and such parts of the land of each delinquent taxpayer to the highest and best bidder for cash as will pay the amount of taxes due by him and all costs and charges. (Sec. 27-41-59). Understand that this is a Tax Lien Certificate sale with right to redeem.

Costs: Costs and fees are not specified by the state statutes.
Redemption Period: Two (2) years. (Sec. 27-45-3). The owner, or any persons for him with his consent, or any person interested in the land sold for taxes, may redeem the same, or any part of it, where it is separable by legal subdivisions of not less than forty (40) acres, or any undivided interest in it, at any time within two (2) years after the day of sale (Sec. 27-45-3).

Deed Assigned at Foreclosure to: Tax lien certificate holder (Sec. 27-45-23). When the period of redemption has expired, the chancery clerk shall, on demand, execute deeds of conveyance to individuals purchasing lands at tax sales (Sec. 27-45-23).

Note: According to (Sec. 27-41-77) the overbid does not draw interest. Furthermore, the overbid will not be returned upon redemption and "shall be credited to the county general fund".

Missouri

Info for Missouri: This Tax lien State has a redemption period of 1 year with an interest rate of 10%. This one is a little trickier.

The way the interest is calculated in Missouri varies based on the amount you pay for the Tax Lien and the time the property is redeemed. Check out our Tax Lien and Deed Master Program for more information.

Summary: In every county all lands and lots on which taxes are delinquent and unpaid are subject to sale to discharge the lien for the delinquent and unpaid taxes as provided for in this chapter on the fourth Monday in August of each year (Sec. 140.150). The minimum bid is the amount of delinquent property taxes, interest, penalties, and costs for the least quantity of any tract shall be considered the

purchaser of such quantity (Sec.
140.190) If there is no minimum bid then the tracts of land or lots shall be again offered for sale, at the next sale of delinquent lands and lots as in this law provided, if the lands or lots are at that time delinquent. (Sec.140.240). After payment shall have been made the county collector shall give the tax sale purchaser a certificate in writing, to be designated as a certificate of purchase (Sec. 140.290). However, if the property is not sold at the first two auctions, a purchaser at a third or later auction receives a deed to the property that is subject to a 90 day right of redemption (Sec. 140.250).

Law: Missouri Revised Statutes, Chapter 140, "Collection of Delinquent Taxes Generally," and Chapter 141, "Delinquent Taxes — First Class Counties and St. Louis City."

Contact: County tax collector (Sec. 140.010). "All real estate upon which the taxes remain unpaid on the first day of January, annually, are delinquent, and the county collector shall enforce the lien of the state thereon."

Interest Rate: 10% per annum (8% on subsequent taxes) (Sec. 140.340). "The owner or occupant of any land or lot sold for taxes, or any other persons having an interest therein, may redeem the same at any time during the one year next ensuing, in the following manner: By paying to the county collector, for the use of the purchaser, his heirs or assigns, the full sum of the purchase money named in his certificate of purchase and all the cost of the sale together with interest at the rate specified in such certificate, not to exceed ten percent annually, with all subsequent taxes which have been paid thereon by the purchaser, his heirs or assigns, with interest at the rate of eight percent per annum on such taxes subsequently paid, and in addition thereto the person redeeming any land shall pay the costs incident to entry of recital of such redemption."

Auction Type: Tax Lien Certificate (Sec. 140.290). "After payment shall have been made the county collector shall give the purchaser a certificate in writing, to be designated as a certificate of purchase." In addition (Sec.140.250), "A purchaser at any sale subsequent to the third offering of any land or lots shall be entitled to the immediate issuance and delivery of a collector's deed and there shall be no period of redemption from such sales."

Bidding Procedure: Premium bid / highest bid. The Bidder offers to pay the minimum sum for the least quantity of land (Sec. 140.190). At third auctions, the

property is sold to the highest bidder subject to a 90-day redemption period. At subsequent auctions the property is sold to the highest bidder (Sec. 140.250).

Costs: As stated in Missouri statute the fees payable by the purchaser include the cost of printing the delinquent property tax list (Sec. 140.170) and a 50-cent fee for the issuance of the certificate of purchase (Sec. 140.290).

Redemption Period: One (1) year (Sec. 140.340). Generally, the owner or occupant of any land or lot sold for taxes, or any other persons having an interest therein, may redeem the same at any time during the one-year next ensuing (Sec. 140.340). A special redemption period applies for infants, incapacitated and or disabled persons (Sec. 140.350).

Deed Assigned at Foreclosure to: Following compliance with certain notice requirements, more specifically, any person purchasing property at a delinquent land tax auction shall not acquire the deed to the real estate, as provided for in section 140.420, until the person meets with the following requirement or until such person makes affidavit that a title search has revealed no publicly recorded deed of trust, mortgage, lease, lien or claim on the real estate. At least ninety days prior to the date when a purchaser is authorized to acquire the deed, the purchaser shall notify any person who holds a publicly recorded deed of trust, mortgage, lease, lien or claim upon that real estate of the latter person's right to redeem such person's publicly recorded security or claim. Notice shall be sent by certified mail to any such person, including one who was the publicly recorded owner of the property sold at the delinquent land tax auction previous to such sale, at such person's last known available address. Failure of the purchaser to comply with this provision shall result in such purchaser's loss of all interest in the real estate. If any real estate is purchased at a third-offering tax auction and has a publicly recorded deed of trust, mortgage, lease, lien or claim upon the real estate, the purchaser of said property at a third-offering tax auction shall notify anyone with a publicly recorded deed of trust, mortgage, lease, lien or claim upon the real estate pursuant to this section. Once the purchaser has notified the county collector by affidavit that proper notice has been given, anyone with a publicly recorded deed of trust, mortgage, lease, lien or claim upon the property shall have ninety days to redeem said property or be forever barred from redeeming said property. (Sec. 140.405), If no person shall redeem the lands sold for taxes within two years from the sale, at the expiration thereof, and on production of certificate of purchase, and in case the certificate covers only a part of a tract or lot of land, then accompanied with a survey or

description of such part, made by the county surveyor, the collector of the county in which the sale of such lands took place shall execute to the purchaser, his heirs or assigns, in the name of the state, a conveyance of the real estate so sold, which shall vest in the grantee an absolute estate in fee simple, subject, however, to all claims thereon for unpaid taxes except such unpaid taxes existing at time of the purchase of said lands and the lien for which taxes was inferior to the lien for taxes for which said tract or lot of land was sold (Sec. 140.420).

Notes: Charter Counties: According to (Sec. 18 (a)) of the Missouri Constitution any 'county having more than 85,000 inhabitants, according to the census of the United States, may frame and adopt and amend a charter for its own government'. In addition, counties 'which adopt or which have adopted a charter or constitutional form of government shall be a separate class of counties outside of the classification system established under section 8 of this article'.

In conclusion, any county with a population of 85,000 or more may adopt a different process for the collection of delinquent property taxes. Therefore, prior to purchase, contact county officials for the specifics on how delinquent property taxes are handled in that specific county.

Sale to Non-Residents: According to (Sec. 140.190) no 'bid shall be received from any person not a resident of the state of Missouri until such person shall file with said collector an agreement in writing consenting to the jurisdiction of the circuit court of the county in which such sale shall be made, and also filing with such collector an appointment of some citizen of said county as agent of said purchaser, and consenting that service of process on such agent shall give such court jurisdiction to try and determine any suit growing out of or connected with such sale for taxes'.

Subsequent Taxes: According to (Sec. 140.440) the purchaser of the tax lien certificate must pay all subsequent taxes 'that have accrued thereon since the issuance of said certificate' before 'being entitled to apply for deed'.

Furthermore, 'any purchaser that shall suffer a subsequent tax to become delinquent, such first purchaser shall forfeit all liens on such lands so purchased.' A purchaser that permits 'a subsequent certificate to issue on the same property' will receive a notice instructing the investor to 'surrender said certificate' to the county tax collector. At that point the investor will receive what he or she paid to purchase 'shall be paid without interest to such holder of the certificate'.

Web Site: https://befreeuniversity.com **Phone:** 855.5BE.FREE

Applying for Tax Deed: According to (Sec. 140.410) the purchaser must apply for a tax deed 'within two years from the date of said sale' of the tax lien certificate. Failure by the purchaser to apply for a tax deed within the time specified in Sec. 140.410 'the amount due such purchaser shall cease to be a lien on said lands so purchased so purchased as herein provided'.

Montana

Info for Montana: Montana is known to be a lien state however you can find some counties that utilize the deed process.

Summary: The county treasurer shall publish or post a notice of a pending tax sale. (Sec. 15-17-122) On the date and at the time and place specified in the notice, the county treasurer shall, except as provided in 15-17-124, begin the tax sale of all property described in the list required in 15-17-122 (2). (Sec. 15-17-211). The sale is made to the person who offers to pay all delinquent property taxes, penalties, interest, and costs due on the property. If no person pays the delinquent taxes, including penalties, interest, and costs, on the first day of the tax sale, the county is considered to be the purchaser. (Sec. 15-17-214).

Law: Montana Code Annotated, Title 15, Chapter 17, "Tax Sales," and Chapter 18, "Ownership Interests in Land Sold for Taxes."
Contact: County Treasurer. (Sec. 15-17-211).
Interest Rate: Five-sixths of 1% per month (10% per annum) plus a 2% penalty fee (Sec. 15-16-102, Sec. 15-18-112).
Auction Type: Tax Lien Certificate (Sec. 15-17-212).
Bidding Procedure: Premium bid / highest bid. (Sec. 15-17-214).
Costs: "Cost" means the cost incurred by the county as a result of a taxpayer's failure to pay taxes when due. It includes but is not limited to any actual out-of-pocket expenses incurred by the county plus the administrative cost of preparing the list of delinquent taxes, preparing the notice of pending tax sale, conducting the tax sale, assigning the county's interest in a tax lien to a third party, identifying interested persons entitled to notice of the pending issuance of a tax deed, notifying interested persons, issuing the tax deed; and any other administrative task associated with accounting for or collecting delinquent taxes. (Sec. 15-17-121).

Redemption Period: Two (2) or three (3) years (Sec. 15-18-111). The owner or any other party having an interest in the property sold may redeem the property within 36 months from the date of the first day of the tax sale or within 60 days following the service of notice of application for a tax deed, whichever is later. For property subdivided as a residential or commercial lot upon which special improvement district assessments or rural special improvement district assessments are delinquent and upon which no habitable dwelling or commercial structure is situated, redemption of a property tax lien acquired at a tax sale or otherwise may be made by the owner, the holder of an unrecorded or improperly recorded interest, or any interested party within 24 months from the date of the first day of the tax sale or within 60 days following the giving of the notice required in 15-18-212, whichever is later. (Sec. 15-18-111). The certificate holder must apply for the deed no later than 60 days following the expiration of the 36-month period at that point if all taxes, penalties, interest, and costs are not paid to the county treasurer on or prior to the date on which the redemption period expires or on or prior to the date on which the county treasurer will otherwise issue a tax deed that a tax deed may be issued to the purchaser on the day following the date on which the redemption period expires (Sec. 15-18-212).

Deed Assigned at Foreclosure to: Tax Lien Certificate holder. If the property tax lien is not redeemed in the time allowed under 15-18-111, the county treasurer shall grant the purchaser a tax deed for the property. (Sec.15-18-211).

Notes: According to (Sec. 15-18-212) 'not more than 60 days prior to and not more than 60 days following the expiration of the redemption period…' the purchaser or assignee 'shall notify all persons considered interested parties in the property, if any, that a tax deed will be issued to the purchaser or assignee unless the property tax lien is redeemed prior to the expiration date of the redemption period…'.

If the purchaser or assignee fails to notify all persons considered interested parties in the property as defined in Sec. 15-18-212 New Window 'the county treasurer shall cancel the property tax lien evidenced by the tax lien sale certificate…'.

Nebraska

Info for Nebraska: This Tax Lien State has a 3-year redemption period with a 14% interest rate.

Web Site: https://befreeuniversity.com **Phone:** 855.5BE.FREE

Summary: The county treasurer shall, not less than four nor more than six weeks prior to the first Monday of March in each year, make out a list of all real property subject to sale and the amount of all delinquent taxes (Sec. 77-1802). The person purchasing any real property shall pay to the treasurer the amount of taxes, interest, and cost thereon, which payment may be made in the same funds' receivable by law in the payment of taxes. (Sec. 77-1808). When a minimum bid is not given, the county treasurer shall issue certificates of purchase of the real estate so sold in the name of the county (Sec. 77-1809). If any real property remains unsold for want of bidders, the county treasurer is authorized and required to sell the same at private sale at his or her office to any person who will pay the amount of taxes, penalty, and costs thereof and to make out duplicate certificates of sale and deliver one to the purchaser and the other to the county clerk (Sec. 77-1814).

Law: Nebraska Revised Statutes, Chapter 77, Article 18, "Collection of Delinquent Real Estate Taxes by Sale of Real Estate," and Article 19 "Collection of Delinquent Real Estate Taxes Through Court Proceedings."

Contact: The County Treasurer (Sec. 77-1802).

Interest Rate: 14% per annum. (Sec. 77-1824 and Sec. 45-104.01). Unless otherwise specifically provided, the interest rate assessed on delinquent payments of any taxes or special assessments owing to any political subdivision of the State of Nebraska shall be assessed at a rate of fourteen percent per annum. (Sec. 77-1824, Sec. 45-104.01).

Auction Type: Tax Lien Certificate (Sec. 77-1818).

Bidding Procedure: Bid down ownership interest (Sec. 77-1807). The person who offers to pay the amount of taxes due on any real property for the smallest portion of the same shall be the purchaser, and when such person designates the smallest portion of the real property for which he or she will pay the amount of taxes assessed against any such property, the portion thus designated shall be considered an undivided portion. (Sec. 77-1807).

Costs: The treasurer shall assess against each description the sum of $5.00 to defray the expenses of advertising, which sum shall be added to the total amount due on such real property and be collected in the same manner as taxes are collected. (Sec. 77-1804), a $10 fee for conveying the certificate or deed (Sec. 77-1823) and a fee of $1.00 shall be allowed for notice to apply for deed (Sec. 77-1833).

BE FREE UNIVERSITY

Web Site: https://befreeuniversity.com **Phone:** 855.5BE.FREE

Redemption Period: Three (3) years. (Sec. 77-1837). At any time within six months after the expiration of three years from the date of sale of any real estate for taxes or special assessments, if such real estate has not been redeemed, the county treasurer, on request, on production of the certificate of purchase, and upon compliance with the provisions of sections 77-1801 to 77-1863, shall execute and deliver to the purchaser or his or her heirs or assigns a deed of conveyance for the real estate described in such certificate (Sec. 77-1837). The owner or occupant of any real property sold for taxes or any person having a lien thereupon or interest therein may redeem the same at any time before the delivery of tax deed by the county treasurer (Sec. 77-1824).

Exceptions to the above include the real property of minors, or any interest they may have in any real property sold for taxes, may be redeemed at any time during the time of redemption above described or at any time before such minor becomes of age and during two years thereafter. (Sec. 77-1826) The real property of persons with mental retardation or a mental disorder so sold, or any interest they may have in real property sold for taxes, may be redeemed at any time within five years after such sale. (Sec. 77-1827).

Alternatively, the purchaser of a tax lien certificate may bring a foreclosure action within six months after the expiration of three years from the date of sale of any real estate for delinquent property taxes (Sec. 77-1902). Any person entitled to redeem real property may do so at any time after the decree of foreclosure and before the final confirmation of the sale by paying to the clerk of the district court the amount found due against the property (Sec. 77-1917).

Deed Assigned at Foreclosure to: Tax lien certificate holder. More specifically, At any time within six months after the expiration of three years from the date of sale of any real estate for taxes or special assessments, if such real estate has not been redeemed, the county treasurer, on request, on production of the certificate of purchase, and upon compliance with the provisions of sections 77-1801 to 77-1863, shall execute and deliver to the purchaser or his or her heirs or assigns a deed of conveyance for the real estate described in such certificate. (Sec. 77-1837).

<u>New Jersey</u>

Info for New Jersey: This Tax Lien State has a redemption period of 2 years with

an 18% interest rate.

New Jersey has a 10-day grace period where the property owner can redeem within 10 days. New Jersey also utilize OTC, "Over the Counter", where you can find some great deals but it will take some digging to find gold.

Summary: Local tax collectors (municipal level) conduct public oral bid tax sale auctions to sell properties having delinquent real estate property taxes (Sec. 54:5-19, Sec. 54:5-31). The property shall be struck off and sold to the bidder who offers to pay the amount of such taxes, assessments or charges, plus the highest amount of premium. Whenever the governing body of a municipality shall by resolution determine that a particular parcel or parcels of real estate, scheduled to be sold at public auction pursuant to the tax sale law, would be useful for a public purpose, it may authorize and direct a municipal official to attend the auction and bid for such parcel or parcels at such sale on behalf of the municipality in the same manner as any other bidder. (Sec.54:5-30.1). If there are no bidders, the property will be stricken off and sold to the municipality (Sec. 54:5-34).

Law: New Jersey Revised Statutes, Title 54, Subtitle 2, Chapter 5, "Tax Sale Law."

Contact: Local tax collector (Sec. 54:5-19). "When unpaid taxes or any municipal lien, or part thereof, on real property, remains in arrears on the 11th day of the eleventh month in the fiscal year when the same became in arrears, the collector or other officer charged by law in the municipality with that duty, shall enforce the lien by selling the property in the manner set forth in this article, provided that the sale is conducted no earlier than in the last month of the fiscal year."

Interest Rate: 18% per annum and 4%-6% penalty depending on the amount of the certificate (Sec. 54:5-61). According to (Sec. 54:5-32), "The sale shall be made in fee to such person as will purchase the property, subject to redemption at the lowest rate of interest, but in no case in excess of 18% per annum. If at the sale a person shall offer to purchase subject to redemption at a rate of interest less than 1%, he may, in lieu of any rate of interest to redeem, offer a premium over and above the amount of taxes, assessments or other charges, as in this chapter specified, due the municipality, and the property shall be struck off and sold to the bidder who offers to pay the amount of such taxes, assessments or charges, plus the highest amount of premium." Furthermore (Sec. 54:5-61.), "The holder of the tax title shall be entitled to fees and expenses in ascertaining the persons interested in the premises sold, but

Web Site: https://befreeuniversity.com **Phone:** 855.5BE.FREE

such fees and expenses shall not exceed in all the sum of twelve dollars, and the holder shall also be entitled for his expenses, to such sums as he may have actually paid for recording the certificate. In addition, and upon compliance with the provisions of R.S.54:5-62 the holder

shall also be entitled for his expenses, to such sums as he may have actually paid for necessary advertising in a newspaper under this chapter and fees for services of notices necessarily and actually served. Such fees and expenses shall be separate, apart from and in addition to those fees permitted under section 7 of P.L.1965, c.187 (C.54:5-97.1) and R.S.54:5-98. Upon redemption in accordance with R.S.54:5-58, R.S.54:5-59 and R.S.54:5-60 the holder of the tax title shall be entitled to collect from the owner or other persons having a right of redemption pursuant to R.S.54:5-54, additional sums in accordance with the following schedule: When the tax title certificate amount shall exceed the sum of two hundred dollars, the holder, upon redemption of the tax title shall be entitled to collect from the owner or other person having an interest in the lands an additional sum equal to two per cent of the amount so paid for the tax title certificate."

When the tax title certificate amount shall exceed the sum of $5,000, such additional sum shall be equal to 4% of such amount paid; and when the tax title certificate amount exceeds $10,000, such additional sum shall be equal to 6% of such amount paid. This section shall also apply to all existing tax title certificates held by municipalities on the effective date of P.L.1991, c.75.

Auction Type: Tax Lien Certificate (Sec. 54:5-46). "Public auction the sale shall be made in fee to such person as will purchase the property, subject to redemption at the lowest rate of interest." (Sec. 54:5-32).

Bidding Procedure: Bid down interest rate. (Sec. 54:5-32).

Costs: The officer conducting a tax sale shall collect and pay into the treasury of the municipality a fee for all costs incurred by the municipality in holding the sale. The amount of the fee so paid shall be 2% of the existing lien as stated in R.S. 54:5-19 and R.S. 54:5-2, but not less than $15.00 and not more than $100.00 for each parcel sold. The fee shall form part of the tax lien and be paid by the purchaser at the tax sale. If a tax lien on a specific parcel is not sold at a sale, the fee for the sale shall be added to the amount due to the municipality and shall form part of the lien and be paid by a purchaser at a subsequent tax sale. (Sec. 54:5-38).

 **BE FREE** UNIVERSITY   **Web Site:** https://befreeuniversity.com   **Phone:** 855.5BE.FREE

Redemption Period: Two (2) years. (Sec. 54:5-86). Except as hereinafter provided, the owner, his heirs, holder of any prior outstanding tax lien certificate, mortgagee, or occupant of land sold for municipal taxes, assessment for benefits pursuant to R.S.54:5-7 or other municipal charges, may redeem it at any time until the right to redeem has been cut off in the manner in this chapter set forth, by paying to the collector, or to the collector of delinquent taxes on lands of the municipality where the land is situate, for the use of the purchaser, his heirs or assigns, the amount required for redemption as hereinafter set forth. When the municipality is the purchaser of a tax sale certificate, the municipality, or its assignee or transferee, may, at any time after the expiration of the term of six months from the date of sale, institute an action to foreclose the right of redemption. Except as provided in subsection a. of section 39 of P.L.1996, c.62 (C.55:19-58), for all other persons that do not acquire a tax sale certificate from a municipality, an action to foreclose the right of redemption may be instituted at any time after the expiration of the term of two years from the date of sale of the tax sale certificate. On instituting the action, the right to redeem shall exist and continue until barred by the judgment of the Superior Court. (Sec. 54:5-54, Sec. 54:5-86).

(Sec. 54:5-61.) The holder of the tax title shall be entitled to fees and expenses in ascertaining the persons interested in the premises sold, but such fees and expenses shall not exceed in all the sum of twelve dollars, and the holder shall also be entitled for his expenses, to such sums as he may have actually paid for recording the certificate. In addition, and upon compliance with the provisions of R.S.54:5-62 the holder shall also be entitled for his expenses, to such sums as he may have actually paid for necessary advertising in a newspaper under this chapter and fees for services of notices necessarily and actually served. Such fees and expenses shall be separate, apart from and in addition to those fees permitted under section 7 of P.L.1965, c.187 (C.54:5-97.1) and R.S.54:5-98. Upon redemption in accordance with R.S.54:5-58, R.S.54:5-59 and R.S.54:5-60 the holder of the tax title shall be entitled to collect from the owner or other persons having a right of redemption pursuant to R.S.54:5-54, additional sums in accordance with the following schedule: When the tax title certificate amount shall exceed the sum of two hundred dollars, the holder, upon redemption of the tax title shall be entitled to collect from the owner or other person having an interest in the lands an additional sum equal to two per cent of the amount so paid for the tax title certificate.

When the tax title certificate amount shall exceed the sum of $5,000, such additional sum shall be equal to 4% of such amount paid; and when the tax title certificate amount exceeds $10,000, and such additional sum shall be equal to 6%

of such amount paid. This section shall also apply to all existing tax title certificates held by municipalities on the effective date of P.L.1991, c.75.

Deed Assigned at Foreclosure to: Tax Lien Certificate purchaser. More specifically, The Superior Court, in an action to foreclose the right of redemption, may give full and complete relief under this chapter, in accordance with other statutory authority of the court, to bar the right of redemption and to foreclose all prior or subsequent alienations and descents of the lands and encumbrances thereon, except subsequent municipal liens, and to adjudge an absolute and indefeasible estate of inheritance in fee simple, to be vested in the purchaser. The judgment shall be final upon the defendants, their heirs, devisees and personal representatives, and their or any of their heirs, devisees, executors, administrators, grantees, assigns or successors in right, title or interest and no application shall be entertained to reopen the judgment after three months from the
date thereof, and then only upon the grounds of lack of jurisdiction or fraud in the conduct of the suit. Such judgment and recording thereof shall not be deemed a sale, transfer, or conveyance of title or interest to the subject property under the provisions of the "Uniform Fraudulent Transfer Act," R.S.25:2-20 et seq.

In the event that any federal statute or regulation requires a judicial sale of the property in order to debar and foreclose a mortgage interest or any other lien held by the United States or any agency or instrumentality thereof, then the tax lien may be foreclosed in the same manner as a mortgage, and the final judgment shall provide for the issuance of a writ of execution to the sheriff of the county wherein the property is situated and
the holding of a judicial sale as in the manner of the foreclosure of a mortgage. (Sec. 54:5-87).

<u>Rhode Island</u>

Info for Rhode Island: This Tax Lien/Deed State has a 100% interest rate that can be bid down to 1%. In addition, to make things even more confusing Rhode Island investors my bid partial ownership.

Summary: Before the sale the collector shall give notice of the time and place of sale posted in two (2) or more public places in the town at least three (3) weeks before the time of the sale. (Sec. 44-9-9), If the taxes are not paid, the collector shall, at the time and place appointed for the sale, sell the property by public auction

Web Site: https://befreeuniversity.com **Phone:** 855.5BE.FREE

(Sec.44-9-8). If at the time and place of sale no person bids for the land offered for sale an amount

equal to the tax and charges, the collector shall then and there make public declaration of the fact; and, if no bid equal to the tax and charges is then made, the collector shall give public notice that the collector purchases for the town (Sec. 44-9-14). The collector shall execute and deliver to the private purchaser a deed of the land, stating the cause of sale, the price for which the land was sold, the places where the notices were posted, the name of the newspaper in which the advertisement of the sale was published, and the residence of the grantee. The deed shall convey the land to the purchaser, subject to the right of redemption. (Sec. 44-9-12).

Law: General Laws of Rhode Island, Title 44, Chapter 9, "Tax Sales."

Contact: Local Tax Collector. (Sec. 44-9-7). The collector may advertise and take, or sell any real estate liable for taxes in the manner directed. (Sec. 44-9-7).

Interest Rate: Ten (10%) penalty if redeemed within six (6) months of the date of sale, and an additional one (1%) percent penalty for each succeeding month. (Sec. 44-9-19) and (Sec. 44-9-21).

Specifically, (a) Any person having an interest in land sold for nonpayment of taxes, or his or her heirs or assigns, at any time prior to the filing of a petition for foreclosure under § 44-9-25, if the land has been purchased by the city or town and has not been assigned, may redeem the land by paying or tendering to the treasurer the sum for which the real estate was purchased, plus a penalty which shall be ten percent (10%) of the purchase price if redeemed within six (6) months after the date of the collector's sale, and an additional one percent (1%) of the purchase price for each succeeding month, together with all charges lawfully added for intervening taxes, which have been paid to the municipality, plus interest thereon at a rate of one percent (1%) per month, and expenses assessed subsequently to the collector's sale. (Sec. 44-9-19, Sec. 44-9-21).

Auction Type: Hybrid Tax Deed. (Sec. 44-9-12). The deed shall convey the land to the purchaser, subject to the right of redemption. (Sec. 44-9-12).

Bidding Procedure: Premium bid / highest bid. (Sec. 44-9-8). The property is sold to the bidder who will pay for the amount of the taxes, assessments, rates, liens, interest, and necessary intervening charges, the smallest undivided part of the land

BE FREE UNIVERSITY   **Web Site:** https://befreeuniversity.com **Phone:** 855.5BE.FREE

which will bring the amount, but not less than one percent (1%), or the whole for the amount if no person offers to take an undivided part (Sec. 44-9-8).

Costs: Costs and fees payable are not specified by the state statutes.

Redemption Period: One (1) year. (Sec. 44-9-25). Any person may redeem property sold at a tax sale at any time prior to the filing of a petition for foreclosure (Sec. 44-9-21). After one year from a sale of land for taxes, whoever then holds the title acquired may bring a petition in the superior court for the foreclosure of all rights of redemption (Sec. 44-9-25).

Deed Assigned at Foreclosure to: Tax sale purchaser. The title conveyed by a tax collector's deed shall be absolute after foreclosure of the right of redemption (Sec. 44-9-24).

Notes: See Sec 44-9-25, Sec 44-9-25.1 and Sec 44-9-26 for details on foreclosing.

South Dakota

Info for South Dakota: This Tax Lien State has a 3-year redemption period with a 12% interest rated.

Summary: On the third Monday of December in each year, between the hours of nine a.m. and four p.m. the treasurer shall offer at public sale at the courthouse, or at the place of holding circuit court in his county, or at the treasurer's office where by law, the taxes are made payable, all lands, town lots, or other real property which shall be liable for taxes of any description for the preceding year or years, and which shall remain due and unpaid, and he may adjourn the sale from day to day until all the lands, lots, or other real property have been offered. (Sec. 10-23-7). After the tax sale shall have been closed, and after the treasurer has made his return thereto to the county auditor, if any real property remains unsold for want of bidders, the treasurer is authorized and required to sell the same at private sale at his office to any person who will pay the amount of taxes, penalty, and costs thereon for the same, and to deliver to purchasers a certificate as provided by law and to make out duplicate receipts for the taxes on such real estate, and deliver one to the purchaser and the other to the county auditor as in this title provided, with the additional statement inserted in the certificate that such real property has been

Web Site: https://befreeuniversity.com **Phone:** 855.5BE.FREE

offered at public sale for taxes but not sold for want of bidders, and in which certificate he is required to write "sold for taxes at private sale (Sec. 10-23-12).

Law: South Dakota Codified Laws, Title 10, Chapter 22 – "Collection of Delinquent Property Taxes ", Title 10, Chapter 23 – "Sale of Real Property for Taxes and Assessments", Title 10, Chapter 24 – "Redemption from Tax Sales" and Title 10, Chapter 25 – "Tax Deeds".

Contact: The County Treasurer. (Sec. 10-22-21).

Interest Rate: 10% per annum. (Sec. 10-23-8). More specifically, "no rate of interest higher than ten percent 10% per year is a valid bid pursuant to this section."

Auction Type: Tax Lien Certificate (Sec. 10-23-18).

Bidding Procedures: Bid down interest rate. (Sec. 10-23-8). Before making a sale of lands and town lots on which taxes have not been paid, the treasurer shall offer each separate tract for sale in the numerical order in which it appears on the tax list and receive bids for it. If any person bids the full amount of the taxes, interest, and costs due on the land or town lots, stating in the bid the lowest rate of interest per year at which the bidder will pay the taxes assessed and due against the land and lots, the treasurer shall sell to that person the land or town lots and shall issue a certificate of sale to the purchaser. (Sec. 10-23-8). The bid must be for the full amount of the delinquent property taxes, interest, and costs due on the land.

Costs: The county treasurer shall charge and collect, in addition to the taxes and interest and penalty, the sum of four dollars and fifty cents on each tract of real property and on each municipal lot or group of municipal lots advertised for sale (Sec. 10-23-5). The treasurer shall collect five dollars for each certificate, and five dollars for each deed made by him on such sale, and the fee for the notary public or other officer acknowledging the deed or certificate. (Sec. 10-23-19).

Redemption Period: Depending on where the property is located, three (3) or four (4) years. (Sec. 10-25-1). Any person may redeem real property sold for taxes at any time before issue of a tax deed therefor, by paying the treasurer, for the use of the purchaser, his heirs, or assigns, the sum mentioned in the certificate, and interest thereon at the rate at which the real property was sold from the date of purchase, together with all
other taxes subsequently paid, whether for any year or years previous or subsequent to such sale, and interest thereon at the same rate from the date of such payment; and the treasurer shall enter a memorandum of the redemption in the list of sales, and give a receipt therefor to the person redeeming the same, and file a duplicate of the same with the county auditor as in other cases, and hold the money subject to

BE FREE UNIVERSITY

Web Site: https://befreeuniversity.com **Phone:** 855.5BE.FREE

the order of

the purchaser, his agent, or attorney. (Sec. 10-24-1). In the case of any real property sold for taxes and not yet redeemed, the owner or holder of the tax certificate may conduct, or cause to be conducted, proceedings to procure a tax deed thereon, as provided by 10-25-2 to 10-25-12, inclusive, no sooner than three years from the date of the tax sale in the case of real property located within the limits of any municipality, or no sooner than four years from the date of the tax sale in the case of real property located outside the limits of any municipality, or at any time thereafter within six years from the date of the tax sale subject to the provisions of 10-25-16 to 10-25-19, inclusive. Such time period shall apply equally to the county or any other purchaser of the tax certificate; any assignee of a tax certificate shall take the certificate subject to the time period of the first owner of the tax certificate. (Sec. 10-25-1).

Deed Assigned at Foreclosure to: The holder of the tax lien certificate. Immediately after the expiration of sixty days from the date of the filing of affidavit of completed service of the notice provided in 10-25-8, the treasurer then in office shall make out a deed for each lot or parcel of real property sold and remaining unredeemed. Such deed shall be signed by the county treasurer and attested by the county auditor, under seal, and shall be delivered to the purchaser or his assignee upon the return of the certificate of tax sale. The treasurer shall receive one dollar for each deed made by him on such sales, but any number of parcels of real property bought by one person may be included in one deed, as the holder may desire. (Sec. 10-25-11).

Notes: According to (Sec. 10-23-28.1 New Window) 'No Sale of tax certificates after July 1, 2006. Notwithstanding the provisions of chapters 10-23, 10-24, and 10-25, no county may sell any tax certificate after July 1, 2006, unless the board of county commissioners adopts a resolution waiving the provisions of this section that prohibit the sale of tax certificates. The county shall be the holder of any tax certificate issued by the county after July 1, 2006, unless the board of county commissioners adopts a resolution waiving the provisions of this section that prohibit the sale of tax certificates. The county treasurer shall continue to serve notice on the owner of record of the real property, publish notice, and attend to the other administrative provisions imposed by chapter 10-23, 10-24, and 10-25. Nothing in this section affects the holder of any existing tax certificate, the method in which the tax certificate is redeemed, or the sale of real property for taxes or assessments'.

Web Site: https://befreeuniversity.com **Phone:** 855.5BE.FREE

Some counties, have adopted a resolution waving the provisions of (Sec. 10-23-28.1 New Window). Such is the case in Pennington County where third-party investors can still purchase tax lien certificates.

Web Site: https://befreeuniversity.com Phone: 855.5BE.FREE

Vermont

Info for Vermont: This Tax Lien State has a redemption state of 1 year with a 12% interest rate. This isn't a prime state to invest in, due to minimal delinquencies, as well as minimal properties going to a tax sale.

Again, if you live close, or are curious, call them up and see what they have to offer.

Summary: The local tax collector may sell real estate to collect delinquent property taxes, costs, and fees at an oral public auction held on the date and time specified in the published notice of sale (Sec. 5254, Sec. 5255). When the time for redemption has passed and the land is not redeemed, the collector or his successor shall execute to the purchaser a deed, which shall convey to him a title against the person for whose tax it was sold and those claiming under him (Sec. 5261).

Law: Vermont Statutes, Title 32, Chapter 133, Subchapter 9, Article 5, "Sale of Real Estate."

Contact: Tax Collector. (Sec. 5252).

Interest Rate: 12% per annum. (Sec. 5260). More specifically, when the owner or mortgagee of lands sold for taxes, his representatives or assigns, within one year from the day of sale, pays or tenders to the collector who made the sale or in the case of his death or removal from the town where the land lies, to the town clerk of such town, the sum for which the land was sold with interest thereon calculated at a rate of one percent per month or fraction thereof from the day of sale to the day of payment, a deed of the land shall not be made to the purchaser, but the money paid or tendered by the owner or mortgagee, his representatives or assigns, to the collector or town clerk shall be paid over to such purchaser on demand. (Sec. 5260).

Auction Type: Tax Lien Certificate. (Sec. 5260). When the time for redemption has passed and the land is not redeemed, the collector or his successor shall execute to the purchaser a deed, which shall convey to him a title against the person for whose tax it was sold and those claiming under him. (Sec. 5260, 5261).

Bidding Procedure: Premium bid up. (Sec. 5255). The property may be purchased by the local taxing district if a bid for the minimum amount is not made (Sec. 5259).

Costs: Include amounts for seizing the property, publishing notices, and conducting the sale (Sec. 5258).

Redemption Period: One (1) year. (Sec. 5260). The owner or any parties with interest in the property sold at a tax sale may redeem the property within one year of the date of the sale (Sec. 5260).

Deed Assigned at Foreclosure to: The purchaser at the tax sale. When the time for redemption has passed and the land is not redeemed, the collector or his successor shall execute to the purchaser a deed, which shall convey to him a title against the person for whose tax it was sold and those claiming under him. (Sec. 5261).

West Virginia

Info for West Virginia: West Virginia is considered a lien state with a 12% a year interest rate and a 17-month redemption period

Summary: On or before the tenth day of September of each year, the sheriff shall prepare a list of delinquent lands, which shall include all real estate in his county remaining delinquent as of the first day of September. The tax lien on each unredeemed tract or lot, shall be sold by the sheriff, at public auction to the highest bidder, between the hours of nine in the morning and four in the afternoon (Sec. 11A-2-10, Sec. 11A-3-2). The public tax sale auction must be held after October 14, but before November 23 (Sec. 11A-3-5). Land for which the minimum bid is not received is held over for a later public tax sale auction (Sec. 11A-3-8).

Law: West Virginia Code, Chapter 4A, "Collection and Enforcement of Property Taxes."

Contact: County Tax Collector (usually, the sheriff). (Sec. 11A-1-4).

Interest Rate: 12% per annum. (Sec. 11A-3-23). More specifically, in order to redeem, he or she shall pay to the clerk of the county commission the following amounts: (1) An amount equal to the taxes, interest and charges due on the date of the sale, with interest at the rate of one percent per month from the date of sale; (2) all other taxes which have since been paid by the purchaser, his or her heirs or assigns, with interest at the rate of one percent per month from the date of payment (Sec. 11A-3-23).

Auction Type: Tax Lien Certificate (Sec. 11A-2-10).

Bidding Procedures: Premium bid / highest bid. (Sec. 11A-3-2). The tax lien on each unredeemed tract or lot, shall be sold by the sheriff, at public auction to the highest bidder, between the hours of nine in the morning and four in the afternoon (Sec. 11A-3-2).

Costs: To cover the costs of preparing, publishing and posting the delinquent lists, a charge of $10.00 shall be added to the taxes and interest already due on each item listed. (Sec. 11A-2-13), To cover the cost of preparing and publishing the second delinquent list, a charge of $12.50 shall be added to the taxes, interest and charges already due on each item and all such charges shall be stated in the list as a part of the total amount due. To cover the

cost of preparing and mailing notice to the landowner, lien holder or any other person entitled thereto pursuant to this section, a charge of $5.00 per addressee shall be added to the taxes, interest and charges already due on each item and all such charges shall be stated in the list as a part of the total amount due (Sec. 11A-3-2).

Redemption Period: Eighteen (18) months. (Sec. 11A-3-18). (a) No lien upon real property evidenced by a tax certificate of sale issued by a sheriff on account of any delinquent property taxes may remain a lien thereon for a period longer than eighteen months after the original issuance thereof (Sec. 11A-3-18).

Deed Assigned at Foreclosure to: The tax sale purchaser. If the real estate described in the notice is not redeemed within the time specified therein, but in no event prior to the first day of April of the second year following the sheriff 's sale, the person entitled thereto shall thereafter, but prior to the expiration of the lien evidenced by a tax certificate of sale issued by a sheriff for such real estate as provided in section eighteen

of this article, make and deliver to the clerk of the county commission subject to the provisions of section eighteen of this article, a quitclaim deed for the real estate (Sec. 11A-3-27).

Notes: Redemption: According to (Sec. 11A-3-25 New Window) the premium or surplus portion of the purchasers bid will not draw interest but will be refunded upon redemption.

Applying for a Tax Deed: according to (Sec. 11A-3-19) the investor can apply for the deed 'At any time after the thirty-first day of October of the year following the sheriff's sale, and on or before the thirty-first day of December of the same year…' Which is approximately one (1) year following the purchase of the tax lien certificate.

Web Site: https://befreeuniversity.com **Phone:** 855.5BE.FREE

However, according to (Sec. 11A-3-18 (a)) the tax lien certificate will cease to 'remain a lien thereon for a period longer than eighteen months after the original issuance thereof'. In conclusion, the investor has approximately six (6) months to complete the tax deed process.

Furthermore, according to (Sec. 11A-3-18 (b)) all 'rights of a purchaser shall be deemed forfeited and expired and no tax deed is to be issued on any tax sale evidenced by a tax certificate of sale where the certificate has ceased to be a lien pursuant to the provisions of this section...'

Wyoming

Info for Wyoming: This Tax Line State has a very long redemption period of 4 years with a 15% a year plus a 3% penalty totaling 18%.

Summary: After notice the sheriff shall advertise the property for sale, and sell the property at public auction, without appraisal, to the highest bidder for cash (Sec. 39-13-108). The highest bidder, shall only pay to the sheriff the amount by which his bid exceeds the amount due him under the court's decree. Upon confirmation of the sale by the court, the sheriff shall execute a deed conveying title to the real property to the purchaser in fee simple subject only to the rights of lien holders from junior tax sales. Any person having an interest in the real property may redeem the property prior to confirmation by the court by paying into court a sum of money sufficient to pay all sums owing to the lien holder.

Law: Wyoming Statutes, Title 39, Chapter 13, "Ad Valorem Taxation."

Contact: The Sheriff. (Sec. 39-13-108).

Interest Rate: 15% per annum plus 3% penalty. (Sec. 39-13-109). More specifically, three percent penalty (3%); plus commencing at date of 1982 tax sale, interest on subsequent taxes if paid by the holder of the certificate of purchase shall be fifteen percent (15%) per annum (Sec. 39-13-109).

Auction Type: Tax Lien Certificate (Sec. 39-13-108).

Bidding Procedure: Premium bid / highest bid. (Sec. 39-13-108). The highest bidder, shall only pay to the sheriff the amount by which his bid exceeds the amount due him under the court's decree i.e., taxes, costs and penalties accrued plus

BE FREE UNIVERSITY

Web Site: https://befreeuniversity.com **Phone:** 855.5BE.FREE

interest, accruing penalties (Sec. 39-13-108). If the property cannot be sold for that amount, the property is bid in for the county.

Costs: The following fees, costs and charges shall be collected by the county treasurer to be credited to the county treasury: (A) Twenty-three cents ($.23) per mile for necessary travel and not to exceed twenty dollars ($20.00) for advertising in the case of sale of personal property and not to exceed twenty dollars ($20.00) for advertising in the case of sale of real property to collect delinquent taxes;(B) Not to exceed twenty dollars ($20.00) for issuing a certificate of purchase; (C) Twenty-five dollars ($25.00) for issuing a treasurer's deed to a private purchaser;(D) Not to exceed twenty dollars ($20.00) for issuing a certificate of redemption (Sec. 39-13-108).

Redemption Period: Four (4) years. (Sec. 39-13-108). The legal owner of property sold at a tax sale may redeem the property at any time before an application for a tax deed is filed (Sec. 39-13-109). Following four (4) years from the date of sale the purchaser may apply for a deed; however, the application cannot be filed more than six years after the sale (Sec. 39-13-108).

Deed Assigned at Foreclosure to: To the holder of the Tax Lien Certificate (Sec. 39-13-108).

 BE FREE UNIVERSITY

Web Site: https://befreeuniversity.com Phone: 855.5BE.FREE

Hybrid States

These states are a little trickier to understand than the plain Lien and Deed states, as they are a mixture of both. Hybrid states are the off spring of both deeds and redemption times (come from liens). While they can be a little complicated, they are definitely worth learning about as there are states with major gold mines that utilize Hybrid Tax Sales. These are also known as Redeemable Deed States.

The key component with Hybrid State is that when you purchase a parcel at an auction you are entitled to the actual deed, however there is still a period of time in which the property can be redeem even after the deed has been issued. If the property owner redeems the property many of times the investor will be award their principle, interest and any maintenance of taking care of the property.

Hybrid State List

Connecticut	Delaware	Georgia	Hawaii
Pennsylvania	South Carolina	Tennessee Texas	

Web Site: https://befreeuniversity.com **Phone:** 855.5BE.FREE

Connecticut

Info for Connecticut: This state has a 1-year Redemption Period with an 18% per annum penalty to redeem. Connecticut seems to be moving slowly to a redeemable deed state as more and more counties are moving in that direction.

In Connecticut most of the smaller counties are using the redeemable deed laws however the larger cities have switched to lien laws.

Success Tip: The larger cities and counties have larger investors with deeper resources resulting in a higher price per lien/property. Therefore, if you are just getting started it can be very beneficial to utilize smaller cities and counties to maybe have more success to obtaining a tax deed/lien.

Summary: According to (Sec. 12-157 (c)), "At the time and place stated in such notices, or, if such sale is adjourned, at the time and place specified at the time of adjournment as aforesaid, such collector (1) may sell at public auction to the highest bidder all of said real property, to pay the taxes with the interest, fees and other charges allowed by law, including, but not limited to, those charges set forth in section 12-140, or (2) may sell all of said real property to his municipality if there has been no bidder or the amount bid is insufficient to pay the amount due." Per (Sec. 12-157 (f)), the homeowner can redeem "…Not later than six months after the date of the sale or within sixty days if the property was abandoned or meets other conditions established by ordinance adopted by the legislative body of the town,"
In addition, as stated (Sec. 12-159), "If the homeowner fails to redeem before the expiration of the redemption period "Any deed, or the certified copy of the record of any deed, purporting to be executed by a tax collector and similar, or in substance similar, to the above, shall be prima facie evidence of a valid title in the grantee to the premises therein purported to be conveyed, encumbered only by the lien of taxes to the municipality…"

Law: General Statutes of Connecticut, Title 12, Chapter 204 (Local Levy and Collection of Taxes) and Chapter 205 (Municipal Tax Liens).

Contact: Local Tax Collector (Sec. 12-155). "If any person fails to pay any tax, the collector or his duly appointed agent shall make personal demand of him

Web Site: https://befreeuniversity.com **Phone:** 855.5BE.FREE

therefor or leave written demand at his usual place of abode or deposit in some post office a written demand for such tax, postage prepaid, addressed to such person at his last-known place of residence or, if such person is a corporation, limited partnership or other legal entity, such notice may be sent to any person upon whom process may be served to initiate a civil action against such corporation, limited partnership or entity. After demand has been made in the manner provided in this section, the collector may levy for such tax on any goods and chattels of such person and post and sell them in the manner provided in case of executions, he may enforce by levy and sale any lien upon real estate for such taxes or he may levy upon and sell such interest of such person in any real estate as exists at the date of the levy."

Interest Rate: 18% per annum (Sec. 12-157 (f)). "..if the delinquent taxpayer, mortgagee, lienholder or other record encumbrance whose interest in the property will be affected by such sale, pays or tenders to the collector, the amount of taxes, interest and charges which were due and owing at the time of the sale together with interest on the total purchase price paid by the purchaser at the rate of eighteen per cent per annum from the date of such sale, such deed, executed pursuant to subsection (e) of this section, shall be delivered to the collector by the town clerk for cancellation and the collector shall provide a certificate of satisfaction to the person paying or tendering the money.."

Auction Type: Hybrid Tax Deed (Sec. 12-157 (c)). "(c) At the time and place stated in such notices, or, if such sale is adjourned, at the time and place specified at the time of adjournment as aforesaid, such collector (1) may sell at public auction to the highest bidder all of said real property, to pay the taxes with the interest, fees and other charges allowed by law, including, but not limited to, those charges set forth in section 12-140, or (2) may sell all of said real property to his municipality if there has been no bidder or the amount bid is insufficient to pay the amount due."

Bidding Procedure: Premium bid / highest bid. (Sec. 12-157 (c)). "…such collector (1) may sell at public auction to the highest bidder all of said real property, to pay the taxes with the interest, fees and other charges allowed by law, including, but not limited to, those charges set forth in section 12-140, or (2) may sell all of said real property to his municipality if there has been no bidder or the amount bid is insufficient to pay the amount due."

Costs: Statutory fees include a $4 tax collector fee for sale and a $6 fee for deed (Sec. 12-140).

Redemption Period: 60 days or six (6) months (Sec. 12-157). "(e) Within two weeks after such sale, the collector shall execute a deed thereof to the purchaser or to the municipality conducting the sale and shall lodge the same in the office of the town clerk of such town, where it shall remain unrecorded six months from the date of such sale.

(f) Within sixty days after such sale, the collector shall cause to be published in a newspaper having a daily general circulation in the town in which the real property is located, and shall send by certified mail, return receipt requested, to the delinquent taxpayer and each mortgagee, lienholder and other record encumbrancer whose interest in such property is affected by such sale, a notice stating the date of the sale, the name and address of the purchaser, the amount the purchaser paid for the property and the date the redemption period will expire. The notice shall include a statement that if redemption does not take place by the date stated and, in the manner, provided by law, the delinquent taxpayer, and all mortgagees, lienholders and other record encumbrances who have received actual or constructive notice of such sale as provided by law, that their respective titles, mortgages, liens and other encumbrances in such property shall be extinguished. Not later than six months after the date of the sale or within sixty days if the property was abandoned or meets other conditions established by ordinance adopted by the legislative body of the town, if the delinquent taxpayer, mortgagee, lienholder or other record encumbrance whose interest in the property will be affected by such sale, pays or tenders to the collector, the amount of taxes, interest and charges which were due and owing at the time of the sale together with interest on the total purchase price paid by the purchaser at the rate of eighteen per cent per annum from the date of such sale, such deed, executed pursuant to subsection (e) of this section, shall be delivered to the collector by the town clerk for cancellation and the collector shall provide a certificate of satisfaction to the person paying or tendering the money who, if not the person whose primary duty it was to pay the tax or taxes, shall have a claim against the person whose primary duty it was to pay such tax or taxes for the amount so paid, and may add the same to any claim for which he has security upon the property sold, provided the certificate of satisfaction is recorded on the land records but the interests of other persons in the property shall not be affected. Within ten days of receipt of such amounts in

redemption of the levied property, the collector shall notify the purchaser by certified mail, return receipt requested, that the property has been redeemed and shall tender such payment, together with the amount held pursuant to subparagraph (A) of subdivision (1) of subsection (i) of this section, if any, to the purchaser. If the purchase money and interest are not paid within such redemption period, the deed shall be recorded and have full effect."

Deed Assigned at Foreclosure to: Purchaser at tax sale (Sec. 12-157 (e)). "… (e) Within two weeks after such sale, the collector shall execute a deed thereof to the purchaser or to the municipality conducting the sale and shall lodge the same in the office of the town clerk of such town, where it shall remain unrecorded six months from the date of such sale."

(Sec. 12-159), "Any deed, or the certified copy of the record of any deed, purporting to be executed by a tax collector and similar, or in substance similar, to the above, shall be prima facie evidence of a valid title in the grantee to the premises therein purported to be conveyed, encumbered only by the lien of taxes to the municipality which were not yet due and payable on the date notice of levy was first made, easements and similar interests appurtenant to other properties not thereby conveyed, and other interests described therein and of the existence and regularity of all votes and acts necessary to the validity of the tax therein referred to, as the same was assessed, and of the levy and sale therefor, and no tax collector shall be required to make return upon his warrant of his doings thereunder, except that the purchaser may, within ninety days of the recording of the collector's deed, request in writing from the tax collector, an affidavit which complies with the provisions of section 12-167a. he tax collector shall provide such affidavit within thirty days of receipt of such request. The town clerk shall record such affidavit in the land records of such town and shall index the affidavit under the name of the purchaser as grantee. No act done or omitted relative to the assessment or collection of a tax, including everything connected therewith, after the vote of the community laying the same, up to and including the final collection thereof or sale of property therefor, shall in any way affect or impair the validity of such tax as assessed, collected or sought to be collected or the validity of such sale, unless the person contesting the validity of such sale shows that the collector neglected to provide notice pursuant to section 12-157, to such person or to the predecessors of such person in title, and who had a right to notice of such sale, and that the person or they in fact did not know of such sale within six months after it

was made, and provided such property was by law liable to be sold to satisfy such tax. The fact that the collector may have charged or received illegal fees upon such sale shall not impair the sale's validity. If the person contesting such fees shows that illegal fees were charged by the collector, the municipality shall refund such illegal fees together with legal interest from the date of their payment in accordance with section 12-129."

Notes: You will need to contact the local municipal tax collectors for information on tax sales. The following website contains contact information for all municipal tax collectors: http://www.opm.state.ct.us/igp/ TAXCOLL/tax_coll.html

Connecticut Contacts
number of Counties: Has no form of county government

Delaware

Info for Delaware: Somethings deferrer in this state county by county. Delaware has redeemable deeds with either has a 20% penalty with a 1-year redemption period, or a 60-day redemption period with a 15% penalty.

Delaware has tax sales more frequent than most states. We have found most counties have tax sales every 3 months. When attending this sale make sure you have the full amount of the bid as full payment is due at the time you pay for the deed. And the full payment is all due at the time you pay for your deed.

Summary: A public sale is conducted by the county sheriff for properties having delinquent taxes (Sec. 8725). The minimum bid is the amount of past due taxes, interest, costs, and penalties. The Department of Finance or the chief county financial officer as designated by the county governing body may approve or disapprove the final bid at a sale made by the Sheriff under this subchapter provided that the notice of the public sale includes that such sale is "subject to the approval of the Department of Finance or the chief county financial officer" in the terms of sale. (Sec. 8726). In the event the Department of Finance or the chief county financial officer does not approve the final bid at such sale, the said Department of Finance or chief county financial officer may expose the property to another and as many

succeeding sales as it chooses

Law: Delaware Code, Title 9, Part V, Chapter 87, "Collection of Delinquent Taxes."

Contact: County Treasurer/Sheriff (Sec. 8773). "Every sale of lands and tenements shall be returned by the tax collecting authority to the Superior Court for the county, at the next term thereof, and the Court shall inquire into the circumstances, and either approve the sale, or set it aside. If it be approved, the tax collecting authority making the sale shall make a deed to the purchaser which shall convey the title of the taxable, or of his or her alienee, as the case may be; if it be set aside, the Court may order another sale, and so on until the tax due be collected. The certificate filed, together with the return and deed, shall be presumptive evidence of the regularity of the proceedings."

Interest Rate: 15% penalty rate (Sec. 8758). "The owner of any real estate sold under order of sale or his legal representative may redeem the real estate so sold at any time within 60 days from the day the sale is confirmed by the Superior Court, by paying to the purchaser or his legal representative the amount of the purchase price and 15 percent in addition thereto or if the purchaser or his legal representative shall refuse to receive the same or does not reside within New Castle County or cannot be found within the County the owner may pay the amount into the Superior Court for the use of the purchaser."

Auction Type: Hybrid Tax Deed (Sec. 8728). "If the owner of the property or his legal representatives fail to redeem the property as provided in this subchapter, the purchaser of the property or his legal representatives, successors or assigns may present a petition to the Superior Court setting forth the appropriate facts in conformity with this subchapter and pray that the Superior Court make an order directing the Sheriff, then
in office, to execute, acknowledge and deliver a deed conveying the title to the property to the petitioner; and thereupon the Superior Court shall have power, after a hearing upon the petition, to issue an order directing the Sheriff to execute, acknowledge and deliver a deed as prayed for in the petition. A description of the property as the same shall appear upon the assessment rolls, and a description by metes and bounds where obtainable shall be a sufficient description in any such deed."

Bidding Procedure: Premium bid / highest bid. (Sec. 8779). "After satisfying the tax due and the costs and expenses of sale from the proceeds of sale under this subchapter, the amount remaining shall be paid at once to the owner of the land, or

upon the refusal of the owner to accept the same, or if the owner is unknown or cannot be found, the amount remaining shall be deposited in some bank in the county either to the credit of the owner, or in a manner by which the fund may be identified."

Costs: See the state statutes for a long list of fees and costs (Sec. 8733).

Redemption Period: 60 days (Sec. 8729). "The owner of any such real estate sold under this subchapter or his legal representatives may redeem the same at any time within 60 days from the day the sale thereof is approved by the Court, by paying to the purchaser or his Legal representatives, successors or assigns, the amount of the purchase price and 15 percent in addition thereto, together with all costs incurred in the cause; or if the
purchaser or his legal representatives, successors or assigns refuse to receive the same, or do not reside or cannot be found within the county where the property is located, by paying the amount into the Court for the use of the purchaser, his legal representatives or assigns."

Deed Assigned at Foreclosure to: The purchaser of the tax deed (Sec. 8727). "Any real estate or interest therein sold under the provisions of this subchapter shall vest in the purchaser all the right, title and interest of the person in whose name the property was assessed, and/or all right, title and interest of the person or persons who are the owners thereof, and likewise freed and discharged from any liens and encumbrances, dower or curtsy or statutory right, in the nature of a dower or curtsy, whether absolute or inchoate, in or to the real estate."

Florida

Info for Florida: Florida is different than almost all other states. Florida is Both a Tax Lien and Deed State, with a redemption rate of 2 years. Florida is a bid down interest rate state begging at 18% interest. The interest is bid down .25 bps. For example, the bid will go from 18 to 17.75 to 17.5 to 17.25 to 17; notice that each bid with down by ¼% or .25bps.

Maximum Interest Rate is 18% with a redemption period of 2 years. The interest is bid down in 1/4% steps. Very Competitive Lien state. The Interest can be bid down

to .25%, but when the lien redeems, you are guaranteed a minimum return of 5%. That is a state set minimum return.

This can be a little confusing but you can bid the interest rate as low as .25% however when the lien redeems, the state will still pay you a minimum of 5% as this is a state set minimum return.

Florida is a very competitive state as they utilize online auctions in most counties. This allows investors outside of Florida to be able to participate in Florida tax sales. Almost all counties can be found at www.realauction.com.

Summary: Per (Sec. 197.432), "On the day and approximately at the time designated in the notice of the sale, the tax collector shall commence the sale of tax certificates on those lands on which taxes have not been paid, and he or she shall continue the sale from day to day until each certificate is sold to pay the taxes, interest, costs, and charges on the parcel described in the certificate. In case there are no bidders, the certificate shall be issued to the county. The tax collector shall offer all certificates on the lands as they are assessed."

Law: Florida Statutes, Title XIV, Chapter 197, "Tax Collections, Sales, and Liens."

Contact: County tax collector (Sec. 197.332). "The tax collector has the authority and obligation to collect all taxes as shown on the tax roll by the date of delinquency or to collect delinquent taxes, interest, and costs, by sale of tax certificates on real property and by seizure and sale of personal property. The tax collector shall be allowed to collect reasonable attorney's fees and court costs in actions on proceedings to recover delinquent taxes, interest, and costs."

Interest Rate: 18% per annum, 5% minimum (Sec. 197.172). "Real estate property taxes shall bear interest at the rate of 18 percent per annum from the date of delinquency until a tax lien certificate is sold."

Auction Type: Tax Lien Certificate (Sec. 197.432) and Tax Deed (Sec. 197.502). "On the day and approximately at the time designated in the notice of the sale, the tax collector shall commence the sale of tax certificates on those lands on which taxes have not been paid, and he or she shall continue the sale from day to day until

BE FREE UNIVERSITY

Web Site: https://befreeuniversity.com **Phone**: 855.5BE.FREE each certificate is sold to pay the taxes, interest, costs, and charges on the parcel described in the certificate."

Furthermore, (Sec. 197.502). "(1) The holder of any tax certificate, other than the county, at any time after 2 years have elapsed since April 1 of the year of issuance of the tax certificate and before the expiration of 7 years from the date of issuance, may file the certificate and an application for a tax deed with the tax collector of the county where the lands described in the certificate are located. The application may be made on the entire parcel of property or any part thereof which is capable of being readily separated from the whole. The tax collector shall be allowed a tax deed application fee of $75."

In addition, (Sec. 197.502). "(5) (c) The clerk shall advertise and administer the sale and receive such fees for the issuance of the deed and sale of the property as are provided in s. 28.24." \

Bidding Procedure: Bid down interest rate. (Sec. 197.432). "Each certificate shall be struck off to the person who will pay the taxes, interest, costs, and charges and will demand the lowest rate of interest, not in excess of the maximum rate of interest allowed by this chapter. The tax collector shall accept bids in even increments and in fractional interest rate bids of one-quarter of 1 percent only. If there is no buyer, the certificate shall be issued to the county at the maximum rate of interest allowed by this chapter."

Going on (Sec. 197.472 (2)), "(2) When a tax certificate is redeemed and the interest earned on the tax certificate is less than 5 percent of the face amount of the certificate, a mandatory charge of 5 percent shall be levied upon the tax certificate. The person redeeming the tax certificate shall pay the interest rate due on the certificate or the 5-percent mandatory charge, whichever is greater. This subsection applies to all county-held tax certificates and all individual tax certificates except those with an interest rate bid of zero percent."

Costs: The tax collector shall receive $2.25 as a service charge for each endorsement (Sec. 197.462). The tax collector is allowed to charge a tax deed application fee of $15 (Sec. 197.502).

Redemption Period: Two (2) years (Sec. 197.502). "The certificate holder is entitled to initiate a judicial foreclosure proceeding any time after two years from April 1 of the year the certificate was purchased; however, the proceeding must be commenced within seven years of the certificates date of issuance."

Web Site: https://befreeuniversity.com Phone: 855.5BE.FREE

Deed Assigned at Foreclosure to: The holder/owner of the Tax Lien Certificate. (1) The holder of any tax certificate, other than the county, at any time after 2 years have elapsed since April 1 of the year of issuance of the tax certificate and before the expiration of 7 years from the date of issuance, may file the certificate and an application for a tax deed with the tax collector of the county where the lands described in the certificate are located. The application may be made on the entire parcel of property or any part thereof which is capable of being readily separated from the whole. The tax collector shall be allowed a tax deed application fee of $75 (Sec. 197.502).

Notes: Florida is unique in that no matter what the winning interest rate is, the investor will, at least, receive a
5% penalty.

(2) When a tax certificate is redeemed and the interest earned on the tax certificate is less than 5 percent of the face amount of the certificate, a mandatory charge of 5 percent shall be levied upon the tax certificate. The person redeeming the tax certificate shall pay the interest rate due on the certificate or the 5-percent mandatory charge, whichever is greater (Sec. 197.472 (2)).

In Florida, once the 2-year redemption period has elapsed and the homeowner had not redeemed, the investor must file an application for the tax deed with the county. Next, the county will attempt to sell the property at the tax deed auction.

The opening bid on an individual certificate on Non homestead property shall include, in addition to the amount of money paid to the tax collector by the certificate holder at the time of application, the amount required to redeem the applicant's tax certificate and all other costs and fees paid by the applicant. Sec. 197.502 (6)(a).

The opening bid on property assessed on the latest tax roll as homestead property shall include, in addition to the amount of money required for an opening bid on non-homestead property, an amount equal to one-half of the latest assessed value of the homestead. Payment of one-half of the assessed value of the homestead property shall not be required if the tax certificate to which the application relates was sold prior to January 1, 1982. Sec. 197.502 (6)(c). The money collected from the sale of the property will satisfy the tax lien including interest. (1) The holder of any tax certificate, other than the county, at any time after 2 years have elapsed since April 1 of the year of issuance of the tax certificate and before the expiration of 7

Web Site: https://befreeuniversity.com **Phone:** 855.5BE.FREE

years from the date of issuance, may file the certificate and an application for a tax deed with the tax collector of the county where the lands described in the certificate are located. The application may be made on the entire parcel of property or any part thereof which is capable of being readily separated from the whole. The tax collector shall be allowed a tax deed application fee of $75.

Georgia

Info for Georgia: Georgia has a 20% penalty the first year and a 1-year Redeemable deed. The investor will receive an additional bump up to 10% every year after the first owner does not redeem.

You will find that most auctions in Georgia are held the first Tuesday of the month on the Court House steps. (Please check with the local tax sales office as this date can change.)

Note: Almost all hybrid states will require the investor to file and go through the foreclosure process which will add more time and about $2,000 to $5,000 in cost to obtain the property. You will need to consider these costs will determining how much you are going to bid.

Summary: (a) Except as otherwise provided in this title, when a levy is made upon real or personal property, the property shall be advertised and sold in the same manner as provided for executions and judicial sales. Except as otherwise provided in this title, the sale of real or personal property under a tax execution shall be made in the same manner as provided for judicial sales; provided, however, that in addition to such other notice as may be required by law, in any sale under a tax execution made pursuant to this chapter, the defendant shall be given ten days' written notice of such sale by registered or certified mail or statutory overnight delivery. (Sec. 48-4-1). The sheriff shall advertise the property for sale in the newspaper in which sheriff's sales are advertised once a week for four weeks before the day of sale. If the taxes are not paid by the day of the sale, the property shall be sold, but only if renting or hiring the property will not bring the requisite amount. Surplus from a sale after the payment of the taxes and costs shall be paid over to the county governing authority as a part of the educational fund, together with a

Web Site: https://befreeuniversity.com **Phone:** 855.5BE.FREE

statement of the property and account of sales, subject to the claim of the true owner within four years. (Sec. 48-4-2)

Law: Official Code of Georgia, Title 48, Chapter 3, "Tax Executions," and Chapter 4, "Tax Sales." Contact: County Tax Commissioners (Sec. 48-4-3). "The tax collector or tax commissioner may place his executions in the hands of any constable of the county, who shall be authorized to collect or levy the executions in any part of the county…"

Interest Rate: 20% penalty (Sec 48-4-42). "The amount required to be paid for redemption of property from any sale for taxes as provided in this chapter, or the redemption price, shall with respect to any sale made after July 1, 2002, be the amount paid for the property at the tax sale, as shown by the recitals in the tax deed, plus any taxes paid on the property by the purchaser after the sale for taxes, plus any special assessments on the property, plus a premium of 20 percent of the amount for the first year or fraction of a year which has elapsed between the date of the sale and the date on which the redemption payment is made and 10 percent for each year or fraction of a year thereafter."

Auction Type: Hybrid Tax Deed (Sec 48-4-1). "The deed or bill of sale made by the sheriff to the purchaser at a tax sale shall be just as valid as if made under an ordinary execution issuing from the Superior court."

Bidding Procedure: Premium bid / highest bid. (Sec. 48-4-1). "For tax sales, property is sold to the highest bidder."

Costs: Not specified by the state statutes.

Redemption Period: One (1) year (Sec. 48-4-40). "Whenever any real property is sold under or by virtue of an execution issued for the collection of state, county, municipal, or school taxes or for special assessments, the defendant in fi. fa. or any person having any right, title, or interest in or lien upon such property may redeem the property from the sale by the payment of the redemption price or the amount required for redemption, as fixed and provided in Code Section 48-4-42: (1) At any time within 12 months from the date of the sale; and (2) At any time after the sale until the right to redeem is foreclosed by the giving of the notice provided for in Code Section 48-4-45."

Deed Assigned at Foreclosure to: The deed or bill of sale made by the sheriff to the purchaser at a tax sale shall be just as valid as if made under an ordinary

execution issuing from the superior court. (Sec. 48-4-6).

Notes: According to (Sec. 48-4-81), "Notice of foreclosure may be served once 12 months have passed from the date of the sale.

Properties that are sold under a tax foreclosure proceeding, the property owner/parties with interest have 60 days from the date of the sale to redeem the property."

Hawaii

Info for Hawaii: This state is a 12% interest rate with a 1-year redemption period. Note: Hawaii auction rules vary per county from the process and redemption periods. You will need to do individual research for each county you plan on participating.

Summary: All real property on which a lien for taxes exists may be sold by way of foreclosure without suit by the tax collector, and in case any lien, or any part thereof, has existed thereon for three years, shall be sold by the tax collector at public auction to the highest bidder, for cash, to satisfy the lien, together with all interest, penalties, costs, and expenses due or incurred on account of the tax, lien, and sale, the surplus, if any, to be rendered to the person thereto entitled. (Sec. 246-56). The collector has the discretion to sell property on which a tax lien has existed for less than three years. The purchaser receives a deed, subject to a right of redemption (Sec. 246-60).

Law: Hawaii Revised Statutes, Title 14, Chapter 246, "Real Property Tax Law."

Contact: County Tax Collector/Treasurer (Sec. 246-60).

Interest Rate: 12% per annum (Sec. 246-60). "…at the rate of twelve per cent a year…"

Auction Type: Hybrid Tax Deed (Sec. 246-60, Sec. 246-62).

Bidding Procedure: Premium bid / highest bid. (Sec. 246-56). "All real property on which a lien for taxes exists may be sold by way of foreclosure without suit by the tax collector, and in case any lien, or any part thereof, has existed thereon for

Web Site: https://befreeuniversity.com **Phone:** 855.5BE.FREE

three years, shall be sold by the tax collector at public auction to the highest bidder, for cash, to satisfy the lien, together with all interest, penalties, costs, and expenses due or incurred on account of the tax, lien, and sale, the surplus, if any, to be rendered to the person thereto entitled."

Costs: (Sec. 246-56) states, "The Investor or purchaser shall render cash, to satisfy the lien, together with all interest, penalties, costs, and expenses due or incurred on account of the tax, lien, and sale, the surplus, if any, to be rendered to the person thereto entitled."

Redemption Period: One (1) year (Sec. 246-60). "The tax collector or the tax collector's assistant shall, on payment of the purchase price, make, execute, and deliver all proper conveyances necessary in the premises and the delivery of the conveyances shall vest in the purchaser the title to the property sold; provided that the deed to the premises shall be recorded within sixty days after the sale; provided further that the taxpayer may redeem the property sold by payment to the purchaser at the sale, within one year from the date thereof, or if the deed shall not have been recorded within sixty days after the sale, then within one year from the date of recording of the deed, of the amount paid by the purchaser, together with all costs and expenses which the purchaser was required to pay, including the fee for recording the deed, and in addition thereto, interest on
such amount at the rate of twelve per cent a year, but in a case of redemption more than one year after the date of sale by reason of extension of the redemption period on account of late recording of the tax deed, interest shall not be added for the extended redemption period."

Deed Assigned at Foreclosure to: The investor/purchaser at the public auction (Sec. 246-56).

Indiana

Info for Indiana: The majority of Indiana is a lien state however it is possible for you to find some deed counties through the state. This is a 10% interest state but can be as high as 25% flat for the first 6 months. Indiana is my favorite state to invest in for several reasons; the interest rate is flat and always double digits, short redemption period, and cash on cash return.

Lien and Deed State. Liens - 1 year redemption period. Tax lien sales are held in

BE FREE UNIVERSITY

Web Site: https://befreeuniversity.com **Phone:** 855.5BE.FREE

August, September, and in October. Deeds - Uncommon, but around. Contact local counties for more info.

Indiana has both online and in person auctions. For more information regarding online auctions, you may find more information at www.sri-auctionsonline.com.

Summary: After the County auditor makes notice of delinquency (Sec. 6-1.1-24-1), each county and certain cities hold annual public oral bids auctions of property on which taxes have been listed as delinquent the county treasurer shall sell the tract or real property, subject to the right of redemption, to the highest bidder at public auction. However, a tract or an item of real property may not be sold for an amount which is less than the minimum bid requirements (Sec. 6-1.1-24-5, Sec. 6-1.1-24-5.2). If a tract or an item of real property is offered for sale under sections 1 through 5 of this chapter; and an amount is not received that is at least equal to the minimum sale price required under section 5(e) of this chapter; the tract or an item of real property may be offered for sale a second time consistent with the provisions of sections 1 through 5 of this chapter or subsection (b). (Sec. 6-11-24-5.5) When a tract or an item of real property is offered for sale under this chapter for two (2) consecutive tax sales and an amount is not received equal to or in excess of the minimum sale price prescribed in section 5(e) of this chapter, the county acquires a lien in the amount of the minimum sale price. This lien attaches on the day after the last date on which the tract or item was offered for sale the second time. (Sec. 6-1.1-24-6).
Law: Indiana Code, Title 6, Article 1.1, Chapter 24, "Sale of Real Property When Taxes or Special Assessments Become Delinquent," and Chapter 25, "Redemption of and Tax Deeds for Real Property Sold for Delinquent Taxes and Special Assessments."

Contact: County Treasurer and County Auditor (Sec. 6-1.1-24-5).
Interest Rate: 10% to 15% penalty (Sec. 6-1.1-25-2).
Auction Type: Tax Lien Certificate (Sec. 6-1.1-24-10).
Bidding Procedure: Premium bid / highest bid. (Sec. 6-1.1-24-5).
Costs: are not specified by the state statutes.

Redemption Period: One (1) year (Sec. 6-1.1-25-4). Any person may redeem the tract or real property sold under IC 6-1.1-24 at any time before the expiration of the period of redemption specified in section 4 of this chapter by paying to the county

treasurer the amount required for redemption (Sec. 6-1.1-25-1). The certificate holder can seek the deed after one year has passed after the date of the sale: (Sec. 6-1.1-25-4, Sec. 6-1.1-25-4.5) but not later than six (6) months after the expiration of the period of redemption (IC 6-1.1-25-4.6). A special 120-day redemption period applies to property sold to a purchasing agency and to property listed on the property lists of consolidated counties.

Deed Assigned at Foreclosure to: The Tax Lien Certificate holder (Sec. 6-1.1-25-4). Furthermore, "A tax deed executed under this chapter vests in the grantee an estate in fee simple absolute, free and clear of all liens and encumbrances created or suffered before or after the tax sale except those liens granted priority under federal law and the lien of the state or a political subdivision for taxes and special assessments which accrue
subsequent to the sale and which are not removed under subsection."

Notes: The tax lien certificate holder will receive a 10% to 15% penalty, depending on when the home owner exercises his or her right to redeem. According to (Sec. 6-1.1-25-2) when redeemed, the home owner will have to pay as follows:
For the minimum bid (delinquent taxes, special assessments, etc.):
(110%) of the minimum bid if redeemed 'not more than six (6) months after the date of sale; or' (115%) of the minimum bid if redeemed 'more than six (6) months but not more than one (1) year after the date of the sale.'
For the overbid (the amount over and above the minimum):
'plus, ten percent (10%) per annum on the amount by which the purchase price exceeds the minimum bid on the property.'
Applying for a tax deed: According to (Sec. 6-1.1-25-4.6) the owner of the tax lien certificate must apply for the tax deed 'not later than six (6) months after the one-year redemption period has expired.'
Consequently, according to (Sec. 6-1.1-25-7 (a)) if the purchaser 'fails to file the petition within the period provided in section 4.6 of this chapter, that person's lien against the real property terminates at the end of that period.'
In addition, according to (Sec. 6-1.1-25-7 (b)): 'If the notice under section 4.5 of this chapter is not given within the period specified in section 4.5(a)(3) or 4.5(c)(3) of this chapter, the lien of the: (1) purchaser of the property; or (2) purchaser of the certificate of sale under IC 6-1.1-24; against the real property terminates at the end of that period.'
'Notice' according to (Sec. 6-1.1-25-4.5) includes a notice 'not later than ninety (90) days after the date of sale of the certificate' and a second notice 'not later than nine (9) months after the date of the sale'.

Web Site: https://befreeuniversity.com **Phone:** 855.5BE.FREE

Pennsylvania

Info for Pennsylvania: Pennsylvania is listed as a deed state however you may find some counties that tax utilize the tax lien laws. The normal process is redeemable deeds with a 90-day redemption period and 15% penalty.

Summary: In accordance with the Tax Sale law, the municipal Tax Claim Bureau is able to sell parcels in one of four ways (Article VI. Sale of Property.); (a) Upset Sale (Sec 601 – 609), (b) Judicial Sale (Sec 610 – 612.2), (c) Private Sale (Sec 613 – 615), and (f) Repository for Unsold Property (Sec 625 – 630).

1. The Upset Sale is scheduled each September and includes those parcels whose taxes, from two years earlier, remain unpaid or other specified conditions exist.
2. A Private Sale can occur after a property has been exposed but not sold at an Upset Sale. An interested buyer submits a written bid to the Tax Claim Bureau. The Bureau decides whether to accept the bid. If accepted, the bid is advertised in a newspaper. Any one objecting to the sale must petition the court within 45 days to disprove the sale.
3. A Judicial Sale is held at least once each year and can include only those properties that have been exposed but not sold at an Upset Sale. After advertisement, notice to owners and lien holders, etc., the parcels are presented free and clear of all liens.
4. A Repository Sale consists of properties that are exposed but not sold at a Judicial Sale. Any bid on a repository property must be approved by all taxing districts where the property is located (i.e., township borough, county, school). Special sales and redemption provisions apply in Philadelphia, Pittsburgh, and Scranton and in Allegheny County.

Law: Pennsylvania "Real Estate Tax Sale Law" Act 542 of 1947, P.L. 1368; 72 P.S. 5860.101
Contact: County Tax Claim Bureau. (Sec. 5860.601). Interest Rate: Not applicable. (Sec. 5860.607). Auction Type: Tax Deed. (Sec. 5860.608).
Bidding Procedure: Premium bid / highest bid. (Sec. 5860.605). Bidders raise bid above upset sales price (Sec.

5860.605).

Costs: Costs collectible as part of the upset sales price include the cost of publishing, mailing, and posting notices (Sec. 5860.605). The tax sale purchaser must pay the cost of recording the deed (Sec. 5860.608).

Redemption Period: Not applicable. There is no right to redeem property sold at a tax sale in most counties (Sec. 5860.607). However, special sales and redemption rules apply in Philadelphia, Pittsburgh, and Scranton and in Allegheny County.

Deed Assigned at Foreclosure to: Tax sale purchaser (Sec. 5860.608). After the court has confirmed the sale and the purchaser has paid the amount of his bid, it shall be the duty of the bureau to make to the said purchaser, his or their heirs or assigns a deed in fee simple for the property sold. Each such deed shall be in the name of the bureau as trustee grantor and shall be executed and duly acknowledged before the prothonotary
by the director and a notation of such deed and acknowledgement shall be duly entered on the proper records. The deed shall, before delivery, be recorded in the office for the recording of deeds at the cost of the purchaser (Section 608).

South Carolina

Info for South Carolina: South Carolina is a redeemable deed state with a 1-year redemption period at a 12% rate.

Summary: After the county treasurer issues his execution against a defaulting taxpayer in his jurisdiction, as provided in Section 12-45-180, ... the officer to which the execution is directed shall: (a) On April first or as soon after that as practicable, mail a notice of delinquent property taxes, penalties, assessments, and costs to the defaulting taxpayer and to a grantee of record of the property, ... The notice must specify that if the
taxes, penalties, assessments, and costs are not paid, the property must be advertised and sold to satisfy the delinquency (Sec 12-51-40). The property duly advertised must be sold, ... (Sec 12-51-50). The successful bidder at the delinquent tax sale shall pay legal tender as provided in Section 12-51-50 to the person
officially charged with the collection of delinquent taxes in the full amount of the bid on the day of the sale. Upon payment, the person officially charged with the collection of delinquent taxes shall furnish the purchaser a receipt for the purchase money. He must attach a copy of the receipt to the execution with the endorsement

of his actions, which must be retained by him (Sec 12-51-60). (A) The defaulting taxpayer, any grantee from the owner, or any mortgage or judgment creditor may within twelve months from the date of the delinquent tax sale redeem each item of real estate by paying to the person officially charged with the collection of delinquent taxes, assessments, penalties, and costs, together with interest as provided in subsection (B) of this section (Sec12-51-90). Upon the real estate being redeemed, the person officially charged with the collection of delinquent taxes shall cancel the sale in the tax sale book and note thereon the amount paid, by whom and when. The successful purchaser, at the delinquent tax sale, shall promptly be notified by mail to return the tax sale receipt to the person officially charged with the collection of delinquent taxes in order to be expeditiously refunded the purchase price plus the interest provided in Section 12-51-90 (Sec 12-51-100). Neither more than forty-five days nor less than twenty days before the end of the redemption period for real estate sold for taxes, the person officially charged with the collection of delinquent taxes shall mail a notice by "certified mail, return receipt requested-restricted delivery" as provided in Section 12-51-40(b) to the defaulting taxpayer and to a grantee, mortgagee, or lessee of the property of record in the appropriate public records of the county. The notice must be mailed to the best address of the owner available to the person officially charged with the collection of delinquent taxes that the real property described on the notice has been sold for taxes and if not redeemed by paying taxes, assessments, penalties, costs, and interest at the applicable rate on the bid price in the total amount of dollars on or before (twelve months from date of sale) (date), a tax title must be delivered to the successful purchaser at the tax sale. Pursuant to this chapter, the return of the certified mail "undelivered" is not grounds for a tax title to be withheld or be found defective and ordered set aside or canceled of record (Sec 12-51-120). Upon failure of the defaulting taxpayer, a grantee from the owner, a mortgagee, a judgment creditor, or a lessee of the property to redeem realty within the time period allowed for redemption, the person officially charged with the collection of delinquent taxes, within thirty days or as soon after that as possible, shall make a tax title to the purchaser or the purchaser's assignee. Delivery of the tax title to the clerk of court or register of deeds is considered "putting the purchaser, or assignee, in possession" (Sec12-51-130). In all cases of tax sale, the deed of conveyance, whether executed to a private person, a corporation, or a forfeited land commission, must be held and taken as prima facie evidence of a good title in the holder, that all proceedings have been regular and that all legal requirements have been complied with. No action for the recovery of land sold under the provisions of this chapter or for the recovery of

BE FREE UNIVERSITY   **Web Site:** https://befreeuniversity.com   **Phone:** 855.5BE.FREE

the possession may be
maintained unless brought within two years from the date of sale (Sec 12-51-160).

Law: Code of Laws of South Carolina, Title 12, Chapter 51, "Alternate Procedure for Collection of Property Taxes."

Contact: The County Tax Collector. (Sec. 12-51-60).

Interest Rate: Depending on the month of redemption 3% to 12% penalty. (Sec. 12-51-90). First three months three percent (3%) of the bid amount. Months four, five, and six percent (6%) of the bid amount. Months seven, eight, and nine percent (9%) of the bid amount. Last three months twelve percent (12%) of the bid amount.

Auction Type: Tax Lien Certificates. (Sec. 12-51-130). A deed is not issued until the expiration of a one-year redemption period (Sec. 12-51-130).

Bidding Procedures: Premium bid / highest bid. (Sec. 12-51-55). The property is sold to the highest bidder; however, the officer charged with the duty to sell real property and mobile or manufactured housing for nonpayment of ad valorem property taxes shall submit a bid on behalf of the Forfeited Land Commission equal to the amount of all unpaid property taxes, penalties, and costs including taxes levied for the year in which the redemption period begins. The Forfeited Land Commission is not required to bid on property known or reasonably suspected to be contaminated. If the contamination becomes known after the bid or while the commission holds the title, the title is voidable at the election of the commission. If the property is not redeemed, the excess above the amount of taxes, penalties, and costs for the year in which the property was sold must be applied first to the taxes becoming due during the redemption period. (Sec. 12-51-55).

Costs: All expenses of the levy, seizure, and sale must be added and collected as additional costs, and must include, but not be limited to, the expenses of taking possession of real or personal property, advertising, storage, identifying the boundaries of the property, and mailing certified notices. (Sec. 12-51-40).

Redemption Period: One (1) year. (Sec. 12-51-90). The defaulting taxpayer, any grantee from the owner, or any mortgage or judgment creditor may within twelve months from the date of the delinquent tax sale redeem each item of real estate by paying to the person officially charged with the collection of delinquent taxes, assessments, penalties, and costs, together with interest as provided in subsection

Web Site: https://befreeuniversity.com **Phone:** 855.5BE.FREE

(B) of this section. (Sec. 12-51-90).

Deed Assigned at Foreclosure to: The purchaser at tax sale subject to twelve (12) months right of redemption. Upon failure of the defaulting taxpayer, a grantee from the owner, a mortgagee, a judgment creditor, or a lessee of the property to redeem realty within the time period allowed for redemption, the person officially charged with the collection of delinquent taxes, within thirty days or as soon after that as possible, shall make a tax title to the purchaser or the purchaser's assignee. (Sec. 12-51-130).

Notes: Penalty due at Redemption: According to (Sec. 12-51-90) 'the defaulting taxpayer, …may within twelve months from the date of the delinquent tax sale redeem each item of real estate by paying to the person officially charged with the collection of delinquent taxes, assessments, penalties, and costs, together with interest…'

According to (Sec. 12-51-90 (B)) the amount charged to redeem is based on the month during the redemption period that the property is redeemed;
* First three months (3%) percent of the bid amount
* Months four, five, and six (6%) percent of the bid amount
* Months seven, eight, and nine (9%) percent of the bid amount
* Last three months (12%) percent of the bid amount

According to (Sec. 12-51-100) 'Upon the real estate being redeemed, the successful purchaser, at the delinquent tax sale, shall promptly be notified by mail to return the tax sale receipt to the person officially charged with the collection of delinquent taxes in order to be expeditiously refunded the purchase price plus the interest provided in Section 12-51-90'.

According to (Sec. 12-51-130) upon 'failure of the defaulting taxpayer, to redeem realty within the time period allowed for redemption, the person officially charged with the collection of delinquent taxes, within thirty days or as soon after that as possible, shall make a tax title to the purchaser or the purchaser's assignee'.

Web Site: https://befreeuniversity.com **Phone:** 855.5BE.FREE

Tennessee

Info for Tennessee: Tennessee is a Deed State that gives the homeowner the opportunity to redeem within 1 year after deed has been transferred with a 10% penalty.

In Tennessee, The Master of the Chancery Court and Clerk conduct these tax deed sales. The opening bid will be the taxes owed plus the penalty and the court costs.

In some instances, you can be given reimbursement for maintaining the property during that 1-year redemption period.

Summary: As a preliminary step toward enforcing the lien for uncollected land taxes, the trustee shall cause in the month of January a notice (Sec. 67-5-2202). After the publication of notice, the trustee shall deliver the delinquent lists showing all unpaid land taxes to an approved attorney (Sec. 67-5-2404). The attorney shall file suits for the collection of delinquent land taxes, as well as the interest, penalties and costs attached to and a part of such taxes (Sec. 67-5-2405). All such suits and all lands impressed with the lien for taxes, penalties, interest, and costs shall be subject to sale under such proceedings, when the amount due is ascertained. (Sec.67-5-2414).

The court shall order a sale of the land for cash, subject to the right of redemption. At all sales, the minimum bid is the delinquent property taxes, interest, penalties, and the costs incident to the collection thereof (Sec 67-5-2501). Where no other bidder offers the same or higher it is the duty of the clerk of the court ordering the sale to bid, on behalf of the county (Sec. 67-5-2506). The government may sell real property on terms to be fixed in the advertisement at public auction to be held in the county where the property is situated (Sec. 67-5-2514).

Any person who owns a legal or equitable interest in the property sold at the tax sale and creditors of the taxpayer having a lien on the property may redeem the property during the one-year right of redemption period (Sec. 67-5-2701). In order to redeem property which has been sold, any person entitled to redeem the property shall pay to the clerk of the court who sold the property the amount paid for the delinquent taxes, interest and penalties, court costs and any court ordered charges,

and interest at the rate of ten percent (10%) per annum computed from the date of the sale on the entire purchase price paid at the tax sale (Sec. 67-5-2703).

Law: Tennessee Laws, Title 67, Chapter 5, Part 20,21,25 and 27 "Delinquent Taxes", "Tax Lien Generally", "Tax
Lien Sale of Property", "Redemption"
Contact: Tax Deputy. (Sec. 67-5-2001).
Interest Rate: 10% per annum. (Sec. 67-5-2703). More specifically, in order to redeem property which has been sold, any person entitled to redeem the property shall pay to the clerk of the court who sold the property the amount paid for the delinquent taxes, interest and penalties, court costs and any court ordered charges, and interest at the rate of ten percent (10%) per annum computed from the date of the sale on the entire purchase price paid at the tax sale. (Sec. 67-5-2703)

Auction Type: Hybrid Tax Deed. (Sec. 67-5-2501).
Bidding Procedures: Premium bid / highest bid. (Sec. 67-5-2501). Increased bidding occurs when the minimum bid being the delinquent property taxes, interest, penalties, and the costs incident to the collection thereof has been raised (Sec 67-5-2501). In no event shall any tract of land be sold for an amount less than the total amount of the taxes, penalty, cost and interest (Sec 67-5-2507).

Costs: The sheriff shall receive as costs to be taxed against each delinquent, seven dollars and fifty cents ($7.50) for serving all original processes, title examination fees, extra publications, survey fees, environmental assessments and other necessary costs, shall be set by the court and shall be considered as court costs of the tax suit. (Sec. 67-5-2410)

Redemption Period: One (1) year. (Sec. 67-5-2701). For purposes of this part, "person entitled to redeem property" includes any person who owns a legal or equitable interest in the property sold at the tax sale and creditors of the taxpayer having a lien on the property; provided, that once property has been redeemed by the taxpayer, no further redemptions under this part are permissible. The taxpayer may redeem the property regardless of whether any other person has previously redeemed the property during the one-year redemption period. (b) In any county having a charter form of government and having a population of less than four hundred thousand (400,000) according to the 1990 federal census or any subsequent federal census, the taxpayer may redeem the property within the redemption period established in 67-5-2702 for counties having a charter form of government.

Deed Assigned at Foreclosure to: The Tax Sale Purchaser. Upon redemption of property under this part, the person who redeems property shall be transferred the interest in the property that was held by the taxpayer prior to the sale for delinquent taxes. However, any creditor who redeems may proceed to foreclose or otherwise enforce such creditor's lien (Sec. 67-5-2706). A tax deed of conveyance shall be an assurance of perfect title to the purchaser of such land at a tax sale (Sec 67-5-2504

Texas

Info for Texas: Everything BIG happens in Texas including deeds. Texas is one of the most popular states for investors especially in the larger cities. Texas is a Redeemable Deed state with a 25% per half year interest rate. A 6-month redemption period unless it has been stamped homestead, in which case it has a 2-year redemption period.

Summary: Tax Sales occur after notice has been provided to a person, the person's real property is subject to seizure by a municipality for the payment of delinquent ad valorem taxes, penalties, and interest the person owes on the property (Sec. 33.91, Sec. 33.911) or the bringing of a foreclosure suit. More specifically, at any time after its tax on property becomes delinquent, a taxing unit may file suit to foreclose the lien securing payment of the tax, to enforce personal liability for the tax, or both. The suit must be in a court of competent jurisdiction for the county in which the tax was imposed. (Sec. 33.41) The property must be sold for the entire amount owed by the property owner, including taxes, penalty, interests, court costs, and the cost of the sale, or the adjudged value of the property, whichever is less (Sec. 34.01 b). If a bid sufficient to pay the lesser of the amount calculated under Subsection (b) or the adjudged value is not received, the taxing unit that requested the order of sale may terminate the sale. If the taxing unit does not terminate the sale, the officer making the sale shall bid the property off to the taxing unit that requested the order of sale.

A person may authorize another person to pay the taxes imposed by a taxing unit on the person's real property by filing with the collector for the unit a sworn document stating the authorization, naming the other person authorized to pay the taxes, and describing the property (Sec. 32.06). After one year from the date on which a tax lien transferred as provided by this section is recorded in all counties in which the property is located,

BE FREE UNIVERSITY   **Web Site:** https://befreeuniversity.com **Phone:** 855.5BE.FREE

the holder of the lien may file suit to foreclose the lien unless a contract between the holder of the lien and the
owner of the property encumbered by the lien provides otherwise.

Law: Texas Codes Annotated, Tax Code, Title 1, Subtitle E, Chapter 32, "Tax Liens and Personal Liability," Chapter 33, "Delinquency," and Chapter 34, "Tax Sales and Redemption."

Contact: The Collector. (Sec. 43.01 (b)).

Interest Rate: 25% penalty. (Sec. 34.21). The owner of real property sold at a tax sale to a purchaser other than a taxing unit that was used as the residence homestead of the owner or that was land designated for agricultural use when the suit or the application for the warrant was filed may redeem the property on or before the second anniversary of the date on which the purchaser's deed is filed for record by paying the purchaser the amount the purchaser bid for the property, the amount of the deed recording fee, and the amount paid by the purchaser as taxes, penalties, interest, and costs on the property, plus a redemption premium of 25 percent of the aggregate total if the property is redeemed during the first year of the redemption period or 50 percent of the aggregate total if the property is redeemed during the second year of the redemption period. (Sec. 34.21).
A person holding a tax lien transferred (transferee) as provided by this section may not charge a greater rate of interest (to the property owner) than 18% a year on the taxes, penalties, interest, and recording expenses paid to acquire and record the lien. (Sec. 32.06).

Auction Type: Hybrid Tax Deed. (Sec. 34.01 (m)). More specifically, the officer making the sale shall prepare
a deed to the purchaser of real property at the sale, to any other person whom the purchaser may specify, or to
the taxing unit to which the property was bid off. (Sec. 34.01m).

Bidding Procedure: Premium bid / highest bid. (Sec. 34.01). The sale is to the highest bidder that is willing to tender an amount that is less than the lesser of the market value of the property as specified in the warrant or the total amount of taxes, penalties, interest, costs, and other claims for which the warrant was issued. (Sec.34.01, Sec. 34.02). The owner of real property subject to sale may file with the officer charged with the sale a written request that the property be divided and that

only as many portions be sold as necessary to pay the amount due against the property (Sec. 34.01i)

Costs: Costs included as part of the minimum bid requirement include the costs of the sale, including advertising costs, and any related court costs (Sec. 34.01). Other costs are not specified in statute.

Redemption Period: Six (6) months for Non homestead, nonagricultural property. (Sec. 34.21) Two (2) years for homestead, agricultural property. (Sec. 34.21 (e)(1)(2)). If real property that was used as the owner's residence homestead or was land designated for agricultural use when the suit or the application for the warrant was filed has been resold by the taxing unit under Section 34.05, the owner of the property having a right of redemption may redeem the property on or before the second anniversary of the date on which the taxing unit files for record the deed from the sheriff or constable by paying the person who purchased the property from the taxing unit the amount the purchaser paid for the property, the amount of the fee for filing the purchaser's deed for record, the amount paid by the purchaser as taxes, penalties, interest, and costs on
the property, plus a redemption premium of 25 percent of the aggregate total if the property is redeemed in the first year of the redemption period or 50 percent of the aggregate total if the property is redeemed in the second year of the redemption period. (Sec. 34.21). The owner of real property sold at a tax sale other than property that was used as the residence homestead of the owner or that was land designated for agricultural use when the suit or the application for the warrant was filed may redeem the property in the same manner and by paying the same amounts as prescribed by Subsection (a), (b), (c), or (d), as applicable, except that: (1) the owner's right of redemption may be exercised not later than the 180th day following the date on which the purchaser's or taxing unit's deed is filed for record; and (2) the redemption premium payable by the owner to a purchaser other than a taxing unit may not exceed 25 percent.

Deed Assigned at Foreclosure to: The purchaser at the Tax Sale (Sec. 34.01).

Who Is Financial Moses?

George Howard Jr., Financial Moses, is a highly sought-after speaker, author,  educator, minister, business owner and authority of Wealth Creation including but not limited to real estate. In the last nine years, Financial Moses, has had an 80% non-redemption rate, meaning of 10 liens he bids he receive 8 deeds. This has allowed him to obtaining over 100 properties at one time and his students over 3000 properties across the country.

Today he teaches real estate including tax sale strategies to individuals from all educational and professional backgrounds. People from all over the world have attended Financial Moses workshops, conferences, school, and trainings seminars.

Financial Moses has taken many small groups of motivated mentees to Live Tax Sales and taught them each step along the way how to buy property safely, and securely. He proudly boasts that no mentee has ever attended a conference and a tax sale without obtaining a property.

Today, Financial Moses owns Be Free University that teaches all aspect of real estate including the Tax Lien Master Program. Twice a year Mr. Howard allows another group of mentees to join his program. Currently there is a waiting list as each mentorship sells out within hours

Thank you for taking the time to read this guide! If there's anything we can help with, please let us know.

Web Site: https://befreeuniversity.com **Phone:** 855.5BE.FREE

Made in the USA
Columbia, SC
29 January 2024

30872214R00067